Chronicles of I

Vol. 2

From the Eighteenth Century to its Demolition

Arthur Griffiths

Alpha Editions

This edition published in 2024

ISBN : 9789367244418

Design and Setting By
Alpha Editions
www.alphaedis.com
Email - info@alphaedis.com

Contents

INTRODUCTION

The gaol of Newgate may be taken as the type of all the early prisons, the physical expression of manifold neglect and mismanagement from the thirteenth century down to our own times. The case of all prisoners in England was desperate, their sufferings heartrending, their treatment an indelible disgrace to a nation claiming to be civilized. The place of durance was sometimes underground, a dungeon, or subterranean cellar, into which the prisoners were lowered, to fight with rats for the meagre pittance of food thrown to them through a trap-door. These terrible *oubliettes* were too often damp and noisome, half a foot deep in water, or with an open sewer running through the centre of the floor. They had no chimneys, no fire-place, no barrack beds; the wretched inmates huddled together for warmth upon heaps of filthy rags or bundles of rotten straw reeking with foul exhalations. There was not the slightest attempt at ventilation, as we understand the word. The windows, when they existed, were seldom if ever opened, nor the doors; the spaces within the prison walls were generally too limited to allow of daily exercise, and the prisoners were thus kept continuously under lock and key. Water, another necessary of life, was doled out in the scantiest quantities, too small for proper ablutions or cleansing purposes, and hardly sufficient to assuage thirst. John Howard, the great philanthropist, tells us of one prison where the daily allowance of water was only three pints per head, and even this was dependent upon the good will of the keepers, who brought it or not, as they felt disposed. At another prison, water could only be had on payment, the price being a halfpenny for three gallons.

The rations of food were equally meagre. In some prisons almost nothing was given; in others, the prisoners subsisted on water-soup—"bread boiled in mere water." The poor debtors were the worst off. For the felon, thief, murderer, or highwayman there was a grant either in money or in kind—a pennyworth of bread per diem, or a shilling's worth per week, or a certain weight of bread: but the debtors, who formed three-fourths of the permanent prison population, and whose liabilities on an average did not exceed ten or fifteen pounds a piece, were almost starved to death. The bequests of charitable people, especially intended for their support, were devoted to other uses; creditors seldom if ever paid the "groat," or fourpence per diem for the subsistence of their imprisoned debtors required by the Act. Any alms collected within the prison by direct mendicancy were commonly intercepted by the ruffians who ruled the roost. When gaolers applied to the magistrates for food for the debtors the answer was, "Let them work or starve;" yet work was forbidden, lest the tools they used might fall into the hands of criminal prisoners, and furnish means of escape. At Exeter the prisoners were marched about the city soliciting charity in the streets. One Christmas-tide, so Howard says, the person who conducted them broke open the alms-box and absconded with the contents. The debtors' ward in this gaol was called the "shew," because the debtors begged by letting down a *shoe* from the window.

Prison buildings were mostly inconvenient, ill-planned, and but little adapted for the purposes of incarceration. Many of them were ancient strongholds— the gate of some fortified city, the keep or castle or embattled residence of a great personage. Some lords, spiritual and temporal, with peculiar powers in their own districts, once had their prisons, so to speak, under their own roof. Their prisons lingered long after the power lapsed, and in Howard's time many of the worst prisons were the private property of individuals, who protected the keepers, their lessees, and pocketed the gains wrung from the wretched lodgers. The Duke of Portland was the proprietor of Chesterfield gaol, which consisted of one room with a cellar under it. For this accommodation, and the privilege it conferred upon him of demanding gaol fees, the keeper paid the Duke an annual rent of eighteen guineas. "The cellar," Howard says, "had not been cleaned for months, nor the prison door opened for several weeks." Another disgraceful prison was that owned by the Bishop of Ely. One bishop had been compelled to rebuild it in part fourteen years before Howard's visit, but it was still bad. It had been so insecure that the keeper resorted to a most cruel contrivance in order to ensure safe custody. Prisoners were chained down upon their backs upon a floor, across which were several iron bars, with an iron collar with spikes about their necks, and a heavy iron bar over their legs. This barbarous treatment formed the subject of a special petition to the king, supported by a drawing, "with which His Majesty was much affected, and gave immediate orders for a proper inquiry and redress."

Loading prisoners with irons was very generally practised, although its legality was questioned even then. Lord Coke gave his opinion against the oppression. Bracton affirmed that a sentence condemning a man to be confined in irons was illegal, and in "Blackstone Commentaries" is this passage: "The law will not justify jailers in fettering a prisoner unless when he is unruly, or has attempted an escape." In 1728 the judges reprimanded the warders of the Fleet prison, and declared that a jailer could not answer the ironing of a man before he was found guilty of a crime. When a keeper pleaded necessity for safe custody to Lord Chief Justice King, the judge bade him "build higher his prison walls." As Buxton observes, the neglect of this legal precaution was no excuse for the infliction of an illegal punishment. Prisoners should not suffer because authorities neglect their duty. "Very rarely is a man ironed for his own misdeeds, but frequently for those of others; traditional irons on his person are cheaper than additional elevation to the walls. Thus we cover our own negligence by increased severity to our captives."

The irons were so heavy that walking and even lying down to sleep was difficult and painful. In some county gaols women did not escape this severity, Howard tells us, but London was more humane. In the London prisons the custom of ironing even the untried males was long and firmly established. An interesting letter is extant from John Wilkes, dated 1771, the year of his shrievalty to the keeper of Newgate, Mr. Akerman. This letter expresses satisfaction with his general conduct, and admits his humanity to the unhappy persons under his care. But Wilkes takes strong exceptions to the practice of keeping the prisoners in irons at the time of arraignment and trial, which he conceives to be alike repugnant to the laws of England and humanity.

"Every person at so critical a moment ought to be without any bodily pain or restraint, that the mind may be perfectly free to deliberate on its most interesting and awful concerns, in so alarming a situation. It is cruelty to aggravate the feelings of the unhappy in such a state of distraction, and injustice to deprive them of any means for the defence of supposed innocence by calling off the attention by bodily torture at the great moment when the full exertion of every faculty is most wanting. No man in England ought to be obliged to plead while in chains; we therefore are determined to abolish the present illegal and inhuman practice, and we direct you to take off the irons before any prisoner is sent to the bar either for arraignment or trial."

Avarice was no doubt a primary cause of the ill-treatment of prisoners, and heavy fees were exacted to obtain "easement" or "choice" of irons. This idea of turning gaols to profit underlaid the whole system of prison management. The gaolers bought or rented their places, and they had to recoup themselves as best they could. A pernicious vested interest was thus established, which even the legislature acknowledged. The sale of strong drink within the prison, and the existence of a prison tap or bar, were recognized and regulated by law. Drunkenness in consequence prevailed in all prisons, fostered by the evil practice of claiming garnish, which did not disappear till well on into the past century. Another universal method of grinding money out of all who came within the grip of the law was the extortion of gaol fees. It was the enormity of demanding such payment from innocent men, acquitted after a fair trial, who in default were hauled back to prison, that first moved Howard to inquire into the custom at various prisons. As early as 1732 the Corporation of London had promulgated an order that all prisoners acquitted at the Old Bailey should be released without fees. But when Howard visited Newgate forty years later, Mr. Akerman the keeper showed him a table of fees "which was given him for his direction when he commenced keeper." The sums demanded varied from 8*s*. 10*d.* for a debtor's discharge, to 18*s*. 10*d.* for a felon's, and £3 6*s*. 8*d.* for a bailable warrant. The exactions for fees, whether for innocent or guilty, tried or untried, was pretty general throughout the kingdom, although Howard found a few prisons where there were none. Even in his suggestions for the improvement of gaols, although recommending the abolition of fees and the substitution of a regular salary to the gaoler, he was evidently doubtful of securing so great a reform, for he expresses a hope that if fees were not altogether abolished they may at least be reduced. However, the philanthropist found a welcome support from Mr. Popham, M. P. for Taunton, who in 1773 brought in a bill abolishing gaolers' fees, and substituting for them fixed salaries payable out of the county rates, which bill passed into law the following year in an amended form. This Act provided that acquitted prisoners should be immediately set at large in open court. Yet the law was openly evaded by the clerks of assize and clerks of the peace, who declared that their fees were not cancelled by the Act, and who endeavoured to indemnify themselves by demanding a fee from the gaoler for a certificate of acquittal. In one case at Durham, Judge Gould at the assizes in 1775 fined the keeper £50 for detaining acquitted prisoners under this demand of the clerk of assize, but the fine was remitted on explanation. Still another pretence often put forward for detaining acquitted prisoners until after the judge had left the town was, that other indictments might be laid against them; or yet again, prisoners were taken back to prison to have their irons knocked off, irons with which, as free, unconvicted men, they were manacled illegally and unjustly.

Perhaps the most hideous and terrible of all evils was the disgraceful and almost indiscriminate overcrowding of the gaols. It was immediate parent of gaol fever. The rarity of gaol deliveries was a proximate cause of the overcrowding.

The expense of entertaining the judges was alleged as an excuse for not holding assizes more than once a year; but at some places—Hull, for instance—there had been only one gaol delivery in seven years, although, according to Howard, it had latterly been reduced to three. Often in the lapse of time principal witnesses died, and there was an acquittal with a failure of justice. Nor was it only the accused and unconvicted who lingered out their lives in gaol, but numbers of perfectly innocent folk helped to crowd the narrow limits of the prison-house. Either the mistaken leniency, or more probably the absolutely callous indifference of gaol-rulers, suffered debtors to surround themselves with their families, pure women and tender children brought thus into continuous intercourse with felons and murderers, and doomed to lose their moral sense in the demoralizing atmosphere. The prison population was daily increased by a host of visitors, improper characters, friends and associates of thieves, who had free access to all parts of the gaol. In every filthy, unventilated cell-chamber the number of occupants was constantly excessive. The air space for each was often less than 150 cubic feet, and this air was never changed. Of one room, with its beds in tiers, its windows looking only into a dark entry, its fireplace used for the cooking of food for forty persons, it was said that the man who planned it could not well have contrived a place of the same dimensions more effectually calculated to destroy his fellow-creatures. The loathsome corruption that festered unchecked or unalleviated within the prison houses was never revealed until John Howard began his self-sacrificing visitations, and it is to the pages of his "State of Prisons" that we must refer for full details, some of which would be incredible were they not vouched for on the unimpeachable testimony of the great philanthropist.

CHAPTER I
THE GAOL FEVER

The gaol fever the visible exponent of foul state of gaols—Neither sufficient light, air or space—Meagre rations—Its ravages—Extends from prisons to court-houses—To villages—Into the army and the fleet—The Black Assize—The sickness of the House at the King's Bench prison—The gaol fever in the 17th century—Its outbreaks in the 18th—The Taunton Assize—Originated in Newgate in 1750—Extends to Old Bailey with deadly results—The Corporation alarmed—Seek to provide a remedy—Enquiry into the sanitary condition of Newgate—Statistics of deaths—No regular doctor at Newgate—Mr. Akerman's brave and judicious conduct at a fire in prison—The sexes intermixed—Debauchery—Gaming—Drunkenness—Moral contamination—Criminals willingly took military service to escape confinement in Newgate.

The gaol fever or distemper, which originated in Newgate in 1750, was the natural product of unsanitary conditions. This fell epidemic exercised strange terrors by the mystery which once surrounded it; but this has now been dispelled by the search-light of modern medical science. All authorities are agreed that it was nothing but that typhus fever, which inevitably goes hand in hand with the herding and packing together of human beings, whether in prisons, workhouses, hospitals, or densely-populated quarters of a town. The disease is likely to crop up "wherever men and women live together in places small in proportion to their numbers, with neglect of cleanliness and ventilation, surrounded by offensive effluvia, without proper exercise, and scantily supplied with food." It is easy to understand that the poison would be generated in gaol establishments such as Newgate; still more, that prisoners would be saturated with it so as to infect even healthy persons whom they approached. This is precisely what happened, and it is through the ravages committed by the disorder beyond the prison walls that we learn the most. The decimation it caused within the gaol might have passed unnoticed, but the many authentic cases of the terrible mortality it occasioned elsewhere forced it upon the attention of the chronicler. It made the administration of the law a service of real danger, while its fatal effects can be traced far beyond the limits of the court-house. Prisoners carried home the contagion to the bosoms of their families, whence the disease spread into town or village. They took it on board ship, and imported it into our fleets. "The first English fleet sent to America lost by it above 2,000 men; ... the seeds of infection were carried from the guardships into the squadrons; and the mortality thence occasioned was greater than by all other diseases or means of death put together." It was the same with the army:

regiments and garrisons were infected by comrades who brought the fever from the gaol; sometimes the escorts returning with deserters temporarily lodged in prison also sickened and died.

The earliest mention of a gaol distemper is that quoted by Howard from Stowe, under date 1414, when "the gaolers of Newgate and Ludgate died, and prisoners in Newgate to the number of sixty-four." In "Wood's History of Oxford" there is a record of a contagious fever which broke out at the assize of Cambridge in 1521. The justices, gentlemen, bailiffs, and others "resorting thither took such an infection that many of them died, and almost all that were present fell desperately sick, and narrowly escaped with their lives." After this comes the Black Assize at Oxford in 1577, when, Holinshed says, "there arose amidst the people such a dampe that almost all were smouldered, very few escaping . . . the jurors presently dying, and shortly after Sir Robert Bell, Lord Chief Baron." To this account we may add that of "Baker's Chronicle," which states that all present died within forty hours, the Lord Chief Baron, the sheriff, and three hundred more. The contagion spread into the city of Oxford, and thence into the neighbourhood, where there were many more deaths. Stowe has another reference to the fever about this date, and tells us that in the King's Bench Prison, in the six years preceding the year 1579, a hundred died of a certain contagion called "the sickness of the house." Another outbreak occurred at Exeter, 1586, on the occasion of holding the city assizes, when "a sudden and strange sickness," which had appeared first among the prisoners in the gaol, was dispersed at their trial through the audience in court, "whereof more died than escaped," and of those that succumbed, some were constables, some reeves, some tithing men or jurors. No wonder that Lord Bacon, in writing on the subject, should characterize "the smell of the jail the most pernicious infection, next to the plague. When prisoners have been long and close and nastily kept, whereof we have had in our time experience twice or thrice, both judges that sat upon the trial, and numbers of those that attended the business or were present, sickened upon it and died."

The gaol distemper is but sparingly mentioned throughout the seventeenth century, but as the conditions were precisely the same, it is pretty certain that the disease existed then, as before and after. But in the first half of the eighteenth century we have detailed accounts of three serious and fatal outbreaks. The first was at the Lent Assizes held in Taunton in 1730, "when," Howard says, "some prisoners who were brought thither from the Ilchester gaol infected the court; and Lord Chief Baron Pengelly, Sir James Shepherd, sergeant, John Pigott, Esq., sheriff, and some hundreds besides, died of the gaol distemper." The second case occurred also in the west country, at Launceston, where "a fever which took its rise in the prisons was disseminated far and near by the county assizes, occasioned the death of numbers, and foiled frequently the best advice." It is described as a contagious, putrid, and very pestilential fever, attended with tremblings, twitchings, restlessness, delirium, with, in some instances, early frenzy and lethargy; while the victims broke out often into livid pustules and purple spots. The third case of gaol fever was in London in 1750, and it undoubtedly had its origin in Newgate. At the May Sessions at the Old Bailey there was a more than usually heavy calendar, and the court was excessively crowded. The prisoners awaiting trial numbered a hundred, and these were mostly lodged in two rooms fourteen feet by seven, and only seven feet in height; but some, and no doubt all in turn, were put into the bail dock; many had long lain close confined in the pestiferous wards of Newgate. The court itself was of limited dimensions, being barely thirty feet square, and in direct communication with the bail dock and rooms beyond, whence an open window, at the farther end of the room, carried a draught poisoned with infection towards the judges' bench. Of these four, viz., Sir Samuel Pennant, the Lord Mayor, Sir Thomas Abney and Baron Clark, the judges, and Sir Daniel Lambert, alderman, were seized with the distemper, and speedily died; others, to the number of forty, were also attacked and succumbed. Among them were some of the under-sheriffs, several members of the bar and of the jury; while in others of lesser note the disease showed itself more tardily, but they also eventually succumbed. Indeed, with the exception of two or three, none of those attacked escaped. The symptoms were the same as these already described, including the delirium and the spots on the skin.

The Corporation of London, moved thereto by a letter from the Lord Chief Justice, and not unnaturally alarmed themselves at the ravages of a pestilence which spared neither Lord Mayor nor aldermen, set about inquiring into its origin. A committee was appointed for this purpose in October, 1750, five months after the last outbreak, and their instructions were to ascertain "the best means for procuring in Newgate such a purity of air as might prevent the rise of those infectious distempers." . . . The committee consulted the Rev. Dr. Hales and Dr. Pringle, F. R. S., and the latter subsequently published a paper in the "Transactions of the Philosophical Society," containing much curious information concerning the disease. The remedy suggested by Dr. Hales, and eventually approved of by the committee, was to further try the ventilator which some time previously had been placed upon the top of Newgate. Nothing less than the reconstruction on an extended plan of the prison, which was acknowledged to be too small for its average population, would have really sufficed, but this, although mooted, had not yet taken practical shape. The existing ventilator was in the nature of a main trunk or shaft, into which other air-pipes led from various parts of the prison. But these were neither numerous nor effective, while there was no process of extraction or of obtaining an updraught. To effect this a machine was erected upon the leads of Newgate with large arms like those of a windmill.

Nevertheless, throughout the execution of the work and afterwards the air of Newgate continued pestiferous and fatal to all who breathed it.

The gaol fever or its germs must indeed have been constantly present in Newgate. The more crowded the prison the more sickly it was. The worst seasons were the middle of winter or the middle of summer, or when the weather was damp and wet. The place was seldom without some illness or other; but in one year, according to Mr. Akerman, about sixteen died in one month from the gaol distemper. Mr. Akerman declared that the fever was all over the gaol, and that in ten years he had buried eight or ten of his servants. He also gave a return to the Commons' committee, which showed that eighty-three prisoners had died between 1758 and 1765, besides several wives who had come to visit their husbands, and a number of children born in the gaol. This statement was supported by the evidence of the coroner for Middlesex, Mr. Beach, who went even further, and made out that one hundred and thirty-two had died between 1755 and 1765, or forty-nine more in the two additional years. In 1763 the deaths had been twenty-eight, all of them of contagion, according to Mr. Beach, who was also of opinion that a large percentage of all the deaths which had occurred were due to the gaol fever.

Twenty years later, when Howard was visiting prisons, he heard it constantly affirmed by county gaolers that the gaol distemper was brought into their prisons by those removed under Habeas Corpus from Newgate. In May, 1763, I find an inquisition was held in the new gaol, Southwark, upon the body of Henry Vincent, one of five prisoners removed there from Newgate. It then appeared that the Southwark prisoners had been healthy till those from Newgate arrived, all five being infected. About this date too, according to the coroner for Middlesex, there were several deaths in the new gaol, of prisoners brought from Newgate who had caught the fever in that prison. This same coroner had taken eleven "inquisitions" at Newgate in a couple of days, all of whom he thought had died of the gaol distemper. He was also made ill himself by going to Newgate. Again in 1772 there was a new alarm of epidemic. In the sessions of the preceding year there had been an outbreak of malignant distemper, of which several had died. An attempt was made to remodel the ventilator, and other precautions were taken. Among the latter was a plan to convey the fumes of vinegar through pipes into the Sessions' House while the courts were sitting. At this date there was no regular medical officer in attendance on the Newgate prisoners, although an apothecary was paid something for visiting occasionally. Howard expresses his opinion strongly on the want. "To this capital prison," he says, "the magistrates would, in my humble opinion, do well to appoint a physician, a surgeon, and an apothecary." The new prison and the last, built by Dance, was just then in process of erection, and was intended to embody all requirements in prison construction. But Howard was dissatisfied with it. Although it would avoid many inconveniences of the old gaol, yet it had some manifest errors. "It is too late," he goes on, "to point out particulars. All I say is, that without more than ordinary care, the prisoners in it will be in great danger of gaol fever."

William Smith, M. D., who, from a charitable desire to afford medical assistance to the sick, inspected and reported in 1776 upon the sanitary conditions of all the London prisons, had not a better opinion of the new Newgate than had Howard. The gaol had now a regular medical attendant, but "it was filled with nasty ragged inhabitants, swarming with vermin, though Mr. Akerman the keeper is extremely humane in keeping the place as wholesome as possible. The new prison is built upon the old principle of a great number being crowded together into one ward, with a yard for them to assemble in in the day, and a tap where they may get drink when they please and have the money to pay." Dr. Smith states that he had no fault to find with the wards, which were large, airy, high, and as clean as could well be expected where such a motley crew are lodged. But he condemns the prison, on which so much had been already spent, and which still required an immense sum to finish it. Its site was, he thought, altogether faulty. "The situation of a gaol should be high and dry in an open field, and at a distance from the town, the building spacious, to obviate the bad effects of a putrid accumulation of infectious air, and extended in breadth rather than height. The wards should have many divisions to keep the prisoners from associating." Dr. Smith found that the numbers who sickened and died of breathing the impure and corrupted air were much greater than was imagined. Hence, he says, the absolute necessity for a sufficiency of fresh air, "the earth was made for us all, why should so small a portion of it be denied to those unhappy creatures, while so many large parts lay waste and uncultivated?"

Another person, well entitled to speak from his own knowledge and practical experience, declared that the new gaol contrasted very favourably with the old. This was Mr. Akerman the keeper, who was the friend of Johnson and Boswell, and whom Dr. Smith and others call extremely humane. But Mr. Akerman, in giving evidence before a committee of the House of Commons in 1779, while urging that few were unhealthy in the new prison, admitted that he had often observed a dejection of spirits among the prisoners in Newgate which had the effect of disease, and that many had died broken-hearted. Mr. Akerman clearly did his best to alleviate the sufferings of those in his charge. For the poor convicted prisoner, unable to add by private means or the gifts of friends to the meagre allowance of the penny loaf per diem, which was often fraudulently under weight, the kind keeper provided soup out of his own pocket, made of the coarse meat commonly called clods and stickings.

Mr. Akerman had many good friends. He was an intimate acquaintance of Mr. James Boswell, their friendship no doubt having originated in some civility shown to Dr. Johnson's biographer at one of the executions which it was Boswell's craze to attend. Boswell cannot speak too highly of Mr. Akerman. After describing the Lord George Gordon Riots, he says, "I should think myself very much to blame did I here neglect to do justice to my esteemed friend Mr. Akerman, keeper of Newgate, who long discharged a very important trust with an uniform intrepid firmness, and at the same time a tenderness and a liberal charity, which entitles him to be recorded with distinguished honour." He goes on to describe in detail an incident which certainly proves Mr. Akerman's presence of mind and capacity as a gaol governor. The story has been often quoted, but it is so closely connected with the chronicles of Newgate that its recital cannot be deemed inappropriate here. "Many years ago a fire broke out in the brick part, which was built as an addition to the old gaol of Newgate. The prisoners were in consternation and tumult, calling out, 'We shall be burnt! we shall be burnt! down with the gate! down with the gate!' Mr. Akerman hastened to them, showed himself at the gate, and after some confused vociferations of 'Hear him! hear him!' having obtained silent attention, he calmly told them that the gate must not go down; that they were under his care, and that they should not be permitted to escape; but that he could assure them they need not be afraid of being burnt, for that the fire was not in the prison properly so called, which was strongly built with stone; and that if they would engage to be quiet he himself would come to them and conduct them to the further end of the building, and would not go out till they gave him leave. To this proposal they agreed; upon which Mr. Akerman, having first made them fall back from the gate, went in, and with a determined resolution ordered the outer turnkey upon no account to open the gate, even though the prisoners (though he trusted they would not) should break their word and by force bring himself to order it. 'Never mind me,' he said, 'should that happen.' The prisoners peaceably followed him while he conducted them through passages of which he had the keys to the extremity of the gaol which was most distant from the fire. Having by this very judicious conduct fully satisfied them that there was no immediate risk, if any at all, he then addressed them thus: 'Gentlemen, you are now convinced that I told you true. I have no doubt that the engines will soon extinguish the fire; if they should not, a sufficient guard will come, and you shall be all taken out and lodged in the compters. I assure you, upon my word and honour, that I have not a farthing insured. I have left my house that I might take care of you. I will keep my promise and stay with you if you insist upon it; but if you will allow me to go out and look after my family and property I shall be obliged to you.' Struck with his behaviour, they called out, 'Master Akerman, you have done bravely; it was very kind in you; by all means go and take care of your own concerns.' He did so accordingly, while they remained and were all preserved." Akerman received still higher praise for this, which was generally admitted to be courageous conduct. Dr. Johnson, according to Boswell, had been heard to relate the substance of the foregoing story "with high praise, in which he was joined by Mr. Edmund Burke." Johnson also touched upon Akerman's kindness to his prisoners, and "pronounced this eulogy upon his character. He who has long had constantly in his view the worst of mankind, and is yet eminent for the humanity of his disposition, must have had it originally in a great degree, and continued to cultivate it very carefully."

Compter, Giltspur Street, London

Another tribute to Akerman's worth comes from a less distinguished but probably not less genuine source. In the letters of the wretched Hackman (who killed Miss Reay) he speaks in terms of warm eulogy of this humane gaoler. "Let me pay a small tribute of praise," he says. "How often have you and I complained of familiarity's blunting the edge of every sense on which she lays her hand? . . . what then is the praise of that gaoler who, in the midst of misery, crimes, and death, sets familiarity at defiance and still preserves the feelings of a man? The author of the 'Life of Savage' gives celebrity to the Bristol gaoler, by whose humanity the latter part of that strange man's life was rendered more comfortable. Shall no one give celebrity to the present keeper of Newgate? Mr. Akerman marks every day of his existence by more than one such deed as this. Know, ye rich and powerful, ye who might save hundreds of your fellow creatures from starving by the sweepings of your tables, know that among the various feelings of almost every wretch who quits Newgate for Tyburn, a concern neither last nor least is that which he feels upon leaving the gaol of which this man is the keeper."

Life in Newgate, with its debauchery and foul discomfort, the nastiness and squalor of its surroundings, the ever-present infectious sickness, and the utter absence of all cleanliness, or efforts at sanitation, must have been terrible. Evil practices went on without let or hindrance inside its walls. There is clear evidence to show that the sexes were intermixed during the daytime. The occupants of the various wards had free intercourse with each other: they had a reciprocal conversation, exchanged visits, and assisted each other with such accommodation as the extension of their wretched circumstances permitted. Dinner was at two in the afternoon, and when prisoners possessed any variety or novelty in food, they were ready to trade or barter with it among themselves. After dinner the rest of the day and night was spent at "cards, draughts, fox and geese," or, as gambling was not interdicted, at games of chance, which led to numerous frauds and quarrels. Rapid moral deterioration was inevitable in this criminal sty. The prison was still and long continued a school of depravity, to which came tyros, some already viciously inclined, some still innocent, to be quickly taught all manner of iniquity, and to graduate and take honours in crime. It is on record that daring robberies were concocted in Newgate between felons incarcerated and others at large, who came and went as they pleased. The gaol was the receptacle for smuggled or stolen goods; false money was coined in the dark recesses of its gloomy wards and passed out into circulation. Such work was the natural employment of otherwise unoccupied brains and idle hands. Thefts inside the gaol were of common occurrence. The prisoners picked the pockets of visitors whenever they had the chance, or robbed one another. There is a brief account of Newgate about this period in the "Memoirs of Casanova," who saw the interior of the prison while awaiting bail for an assault. Casanova was committed in ball dress, and was received with hisses, which increased to furious abuse when they found he did not answer their questions, being ignorant of English. He felt as if he was in one of the most horrible circles of Dante's hell. He saw, "Des figures fauves, des regards de vipères, des sinistres sourires tous les caractères de l'envie de la rage, du desespoir; c'était un spectacle epouvantable."

It was not strange that the inmates of Newgate should hold this miserable life of theirs pretty cheap, and be ready to risk it in any way to compass enlargement from gaol. Newgate was always constantly drawn upon by those who wanted men for any desperate enterprise. In the early days of inoculation, soon after it had been introduced from the East by Lady Mary Wortly Montague, and when it was still styled engrafting, the process was first tried upon seven condemned prisoners, with a certain success. Again, a reprieve was granted to another convict under sentence of death, on condition that he permit an experiment to be performed on his ear. The process, which was the invention of a Mr. Charles Elden, was intended to cure deafness by cutting the tympanum. Sometimes a convicted criminal was allowed to choose between a year's imprisonment in Newgate or taking service under the Crown. There are also many entries in the State Papers of prisoners pardoned to join His Majesty's forces. Not that these very questionable recruits were willingly accepted. I find on 13th May, 1767, in reply to a letter forwarding a list of convicts so pardoned, a protest from the Secretary of War, who says that commanding officers are very much averse to accepting the services of these gaol-birds, and have often solicited him not to send them out to their regiments. The practice was the more objectionable as at that time the term of service for free volunteers was for life, while the ex-convicts only joined the colours for a limited period. The point was not pressed therefore in its entirety, but the concession made, that these convicts should be enlarged for special service on the west coast of Africa. It was argued that "considering the unhealthiness of the climate, His Majesty is desirous that the troops stationed there should be recruited rather with such men as must look upon that duty as a mitigation of their sentences than with deserving volunteers." But to this again objections were raised by the agent to the troops at Senegal, who pointed out the extreme danger to life and property of sending nineteen sturdy cut-throats armed and accoutred to reside within the walls of a feeble place, having a total garrison of sixty men, adding that, "should this embarkation of thieves take place he would be glad to insure his property at seventy-five per cent."

CHAPTER II
THE REBUILDING OF NEWGATE

In 1762 Press-yard destroyed by fire—Two prisoners burnt to death—It is decided to rebuild—Lord Mayor Beckford lays first stone in 1770—The new gaol is gutted in the Lord George Gordon riots—Origin of these riots—Lord George, at head of procession, presents petition to House of Commons—Mob attracted to Newgate—The gaoler, Mr. Akerman, summoned to surrender, and release his prisoners—Rioters storm Newgate—Sack Governor's house—Rioters, headed by Dennis the hangman, rush in and set inmates free—Other gaols attacked and burnt—The military called out—Lord George arrested, lodged in the Tower, and tried for high treason, but acquitted, and sentenced to fines and imprisonment in Newgate—Dies in Newgate of gaol fever, 1793.

In 1757 the residents in the immediate neighbourhood of Newgate raised their protest against the gaol, and petitioned the Corporation, "setting forth their apprehensions from their vicinity to Newgate, and from the stenches proceeding therefrom, of being subject to an infectious disease called the gaol distemper." Upon receipt of this petition, the Common Council appointed a fresh committee, and the various allegations were gone into seriatim. They next surveyed the gaol itself and the surrounding premises, examined the site with a view to rebuilding, and had plans prepared with estimates and specifications as to cost of ground and construction. The projected design embraced a series of quadrangles, one for the debtors and another for the felons, with an area for each. The probable expense for the work which the committee were of the opinion was greatly needed would amount to about £40,000, for which sum "they did resolve to petition Parliament for a grant." This petition was, however, never presented. Mr. Alderman Dickens, having spoken privately to the Chancellor of the Exchequer on the subject, was informed that no public money would be forthcoming, and the project again fell through.

It did not entirely drop notwithstanding. To the credit of the Corporation it must be stated, that many attempts were made to grapple with the difficulties of ways and means. Application was made to Parliament more than once for power to raise money for the work by some proportionable tax on the city and county, but always without avail. Parties differed as to the manner in which funds should be obtained, yet all were agreed upon the "immediate necessity for converting this seat of misery and disease, this dangerous source of contagion, into a secure and wholesome place of confinement." The matter became more urgent, the occasion more opportune, when that part of the prison styled the press-yard was destroyed by fire in 1762.

Some account of this fire may be inserted here. It broke out in the middle of the night at the back of the staircase in the press-yard, and in a few hours consumed all the apartments in that place, and greatly damaged the chapel. Other adjoining premises, particularly that of a stocking-trimmer in Phœnix Court, were greatly injured by the fire. Worst of all, two prisoners perished in the flames. One was Captain Ogle, who had been tried for murdering the cook of the Vine Tavern, near Dover St., Piccadilly, but had been found insane on arraignment, and had accordingly been detained in prison "during His Majesty's pleasure." There was no Broadmoor asylum in those days for criminal lunatics and Newgate was a poor substitute for the palatial establishment now standing among the Berkshire pine woods. The fire was supposed to have originated in Captain Ogle's room. Beneath it was one occupied by Thomas Smith, a horse-dealer, committed to prison on suspicion of stealing corn from Alderman Masters. Smith's wife the night before the conflagration had carried him the whole of his effects, amounting to some five or six hundred pounds in notes and bank bills. When the fire was raging Smith was heard to cry out for help. He was seen also to put his arm through the iron grating, which, however, was so excessively hot that it set his shirt on fire. About this time it is supposed that he threw out his pocket-book containing the notes; it was caught and the valuables saved. A few minutes later the floor fell in, and both Captain Ogle and Smith were buried in the ruins. The fire had burnt so fiercely and so fast that no one could go to the assistance of either of these unfortunates. About four o'clock in the morning the Lord Mayor and sheriffs arrived upon the scene, and took an active part in the steps taken to check the fire and provide for the safety of the prisoners. By six o'clock, there being an abundance of water handy, the flames had greatly abated, but the fire continued to burn till two in the afternoon, and ended by the fall of a party wall which happily did no great damage. This was no doubt the fire at which Mr. Akerman behaved with such intrepidity, and which has already been described.

After the fire it was admitted that the proper time had arrived for "putting in execution the plan of rebuilding this inconvenient gaol, which was thought of some time ago." Once more a committee of the Common Council was appointed, and once more the question of site was considered, with the result that the locality of the existing prison was decided upon as the most suitable and convenient. The first stone of the new gaol was laid on the 31st May, 1770, by the Lord Mayor, William Beckford, Esquire, the founder of that family.

Within a year or two of its completion, the new Newgate had to pass through an ordeal which nearly ended its existence. Its boasted strength as a place of durance was boldly set at naught, and almost for the first and last time in this country this gaol, with others in the metropolis, was sacked and its imprisoned inmates set free. The occasion grew out of the so-called Lord George Gordon Riots in 1780. These well-known disturbances had their origin in the relaxation of the penal laws against the Roman Catholics. Such concessions raised fanatical passion to fever pitch. Ignorance and intolerance went hand in hand, and the malcontents, belonging mainly to the lowest strata of society, found a champion in a weak-minded and misguided cadet of the ducal house of Gordon. Lord George Gordon, who was a member of the House of Commons, showed signs of eccentricity soon after he took his seat, but it was at first more ridiculous than mischievous. Lord George became more dangerously meddlesome when the anti-Catholic agitation began. It was to him that the Protestant association looked for countenance and support, and when Lord North at his instance refused to present a petition from that society to Parliament, Lord George Gordon promised to do so in person, provided it was backed by a multitude not less than twenty thousand strong.

This led to the great gathering in St. George's Fields on the 2nd June, 1780, when thousands organized themselves into three columns, and proceeded to the House of Commons across the three bridges, Westminster, Blackfriars, and London Bridge. Lord George headed the Westminster procession, and all three concentrated at St. Stephen's between two and three in the afternoon. There the mob filled every avenue and approach; crowds overflowed the lobbies, and would have pushed into the body of the House. Lord George went ahead with the monster petition, which bore some hundred and twenty thousand signatures or "marks," and which the Commons by a negative vote of 192 to 6 refused to receive. After this the rioters, at the instigation of their leader, hastened *en masse* to destroy the chapels of the foreign ambassadors. This was followed by other outrages. While some of their number attacked and rifled the dwellings of persons especially obnoxious to them, others set fire to public buildings, and ransacked the taverns. The military had been called out early in the day, and had made many arrests. As the prisoners were taken to Newgate, the fury of the populace was attracted to this gaol, and a large force, computed at quite two-thirds of the rioters, proceeded thither, determined to force open its gates. This mob was composed of the lowest scum of the town, roughs brutal and utterly reckless, having a natural loathing for prisons, their keepers, and all the machinery of the law. Many already knew, and but too well, the inside of Newgate, many dreaded to return there, either as lodgers or travellers bound on the fatal road to Tyburn. One wild fierce desire was uppermost with all, one thought possessed their minds to the exclusion of all others— to destroy the hateful prison-house and raze it to the ground.

On arriving at the Old Bailey in front of the stone façade, as grim and solid as that of any fortress, the mob halted and demanded the gaoler, Mr. Akerman, who appeared at a window, some say on the roof, of his house, which forms the centre of the line of buildings facing Newgate Street. When he appeared the mob called on him to release their confederates and surrender the place unconditionally. Mr. Akerman distinctly and without hesitation refused, and then, dreading what was coming, he made the best of his way to the sheriffs, in order to know their pleasure. As the front of the prison was beset by the densely-packed riotous assemblage, Mr. Akerman probably made use of the side wicket and passage which leads direct from Newgate into the Sessions' House. The magistrates seemed to have been in doubt how to act, and for some time did nothing. "Their timidity and negligence," says Boswell, helped the almost incredible exertions of the mob. And he is of opinion, that had proper aid been given to Mr. Akerman, the sacking of Newgate would certainly have been prevented. While the magistrates hesitated the mob were furiously active; excited to frenzy, they tried to beat down the gate with sledge-hammers, and vainly sought to make some impression on the massive walls. A portion of the assailants forced their way into the governor's house, and laying hands upon his furniture, with all other combustibles, dragged them out and made a great pile in front of the obdurate door, which still resisted force. The heap of wood, having been anointed with rosin and turpentine, was kindled, and soon fanned into a mighty blaze. The door, heavily barred and bolted, and strongly bound with iron, did not ignite quite readily, but presently it took fire and burned steadily, though slowly. Meanwhile the rioters fed the flames with fresh fuel, and snatching burning brands from the fire, cast them on to the roof and over the external wall into the wards and yards within. The prisoners inside, who had heard without fully understanding the din, and saw the flames without knowing whether they promised deliverance or foreboded a dreadful death, suffered the keenest mental torture, and added their agonized shouts to the general uproar.

Through all this tumult and destruction the law was paralyzed. After much delay the sheriff sent a party of constables to the gaolers' assistance. But they came too late, and easily fell into a trap. The rioters suffered them to pass until they were entirely encircled, then attacked them with great fury, disarmed them, took their staves, and quickly converted them at the fire into blazing brands, which they threw about to extend the flames. "It is scarcely to be credited," says a narrator, "with what celerity a gaol which to a common observer appeared to be built with nothing that would burn, was destroyed by the flames. So efficient were the means employed, that the work of destruction was very rapid. Stones two or three tons in weight, to which the doors of the cells were fastened, were raised by that resistless species of crow known to housebreakers by the name of the pig's foot. Such was the violence of the fire, that the great iron bars and windows were eaten through and the adjacent stones vitrified. Nor is it less astonishing that from a prison thus in flames a miserable crew of felons in irons and a company of confined debtors, to the number in the whole of more than three hundred, could all be liberated as it were by magic, amidst flames and fire-brands, without the loss of a single life. . . . But it is not at all to be wondered that by a body of execrable villains thus let loose upon the public, the house of that worthy and active magistrate, Sir John Fielding, should be the first marked for vengeance." In the same way, even before the destruction of Newgate, the house of Justice Hyde, whose activity the rioters resented, had also been stripped of its furniture, which was burnt in front of the door.

Crabbe's account written at the time to a friend is graphic, and contains several new details—"How Akerman, the governor, escaped," he says, "or where he is gone, I know not; but just at the time I speak of they set fire to his house, broke in, and threw every piece of furniture they could find into the street, firing them also in an instant. The engines came, but they were only suffered to preserve the private houses near the prison. As I was standing near the spot, there approached another body of men—I suppose five hundred—and Lord George Gordon, in a coach drawn by the mob, towards Alderman Bull's, bowing as he passed along. He is a lively-looking young man in appearance and nothing more, though just now the popular hero. By eight o'clock Akerman's house was in flames. I went close to it, and never saw anything so dreadful. The prison was, as I have said, a remarkably strong building; but, determined to force it, they broke the gates with crows and other instruments, and climbed up outside of the cell part, which joins the two great wings of the building where the felons were confined; and I stood where I plainly saw their operations; they broke the roof, tore away the rafters, and having got ladders, they descended. Not Orpheus himself had more courage or better luck. Flames all around them, and a body of soldiers expected, yet they laughed at all opposition. The prisoners escaped. I stood and saw about twelve women and eight men ascend from their confinement to the open air, and they were conducted through the streets in their chains. Three of these were to be hanged on Friday (two days later).

"You have no conception of the frenzy of the multitude. This now being done, and Akerman's house now a mere shell of brick-work, they kept a store of flame for other purposes. It became red-hot, and the doors and windows appeared like the entrance to so many volcanoes. With some difficulty they then fired the debtors' prison, broke the doors, and they too all made their escape. Tired of the scene, I went home, and returned again at eleven o'clock at night. I met large bodies of horse and foot soldiers coming to guard the

Bank and some houses of Roman Catholics near it. Newgate was at this time open to all; any one might get in, and what was never the case before, any one might get out. I did both, for the people were now chiefly lookers-on. The mischief was done, and the doers of it gone to another part of the town. . . . But I must not omit what struck me most: about ten or twelve of the mob getting to the top of the debtors' prison whilst it was burning, to halloo, they appeared rolled in black smoke mixed with sudden bursts of fire—like Milton's infernals, who were as familiar with flames as with each other."

It should be added here that the excesses of the rioters did not end with the burning of Newgate; they did other mischief. Five other prisons, the new prison, Clerkenwell, the Fleet, the King's Bench, the Borough Clink in Tooley Street, and the new Bridewell, were attacked, their inmates released, and the buildings set on fire. At one time the town was convulsed with terror at a report that the rioters intended to open the gates of Bedlam, and let loose gangs of raving lunatics to range recklessly about. They made an attempt upon the Bank of England, but were repulsed with loss by John Wilkes and the soldiers on guard. At one time during the night as many as thirty-six incendiary fires were ablaze. The troops had been called upon to support the civil power, and had acted with vigour. There was fighting in nearly all the streets, constant firing. At times the soldiers charged with the bayonet. The streets ran with blood. In all, before tranquillity was restored, nearly five hundred persons had been killed and wounded, and to this long bill of mortality must be added the fifty-nine capitally convicted under the special commission appointed to try the rioters.

It was in many cases cruel kindness to set the prisoners free. Numbers of the debtors of the King's Bench were loth to leave their place of confinement, for they had no friends and nowhere else to go. Of the three hundred released so unexpectedly from Newgate, some returned on their own accord a few days later and gave themselves up. It is said that many others were drawn back by an irresistible attraction, and were actually found loitering about the open wards of the prison. Fifty were thus retaken within the walls the day after the fire, and others kept dropping by twos and threes to examine their old haunts and see for themselves what was going on. Some were found trying to rekindle the fire; some merely prowled about the place, "being often found asleep in the ruins, or sitting talking there, or even eating and drinking, as in a choice retreat."

The ringleader and prime mover, Lord George Gordon, was arrested on the evening of the 9th, and conveyed to the Tower. His trial did not come on till the following February at the King's Bench, where he was indicted for high treason. He was charged with levying war against the majesty of the king; "not having the fear of God before his eyes, but being moved and seduced by the instigation of the devil; . . . that he unlawfully, maliciously, and traitorously did compass, imagine, and intend to raise and levy war, insurrection, and rebellion," and assembled with some five hundred more, "armed and arrayed in a warlike manner, with colours flying, and with swords, clubs, bludgeons, staves and other weapons," in the liberty of Westminster. It was proved in evidence that Lord George directed the Associated Protestants to meet him at Westminster in their best clothes, and with blue cockades in their hats, and said he should wear one himself. He was also heard to declare that the king had broken his coronation oath, and to exhort the mob to continue steadfast in so good and glorious a cause. For the defence it was urged that Lord George Gordon had desired nothing but to compass by all legal means the repeal of the Act of Toleration; that he had no other view than the Protestant interest, and had always demeaned himself in the most loyal manner. He had hoped that the great gathering would be all peaceable; that the mob "should not so much as take sticks in their hands," should abstain from all violence, surrender at once any one riotously disposed; in a word, should exhibit the true Protestant spirit, and if struck should turn the other cheek. Mr. Erskine, Lord George's counsel, after pointing out that his client had suffered already a long and rigorous imprisonment, his great youth, his illustrious lineage and zeal in parliament for the constitution of his country, urged that the evidence and the whole tenor of the prisoner's conduct repelled the belief of traitorous purpose. The jury retired for half an hour, and then brought in a verdict of not guilty.

Lord George, unhappily, could not keep out of trouble, although naturally of mild disposition. He was an excitable, rather weak-minded man, easily carried away by his enthusiasm on particular points. Six years later he espoused, with customary warmth and want of judgment, the case of other prisoners in Newgate, and published a pamphlet purporting to be a petition from them presented to himself, praying him to "interfere and secure their liberties by preventing their being sent to Botany Bay. Prisoners labouring under severe sentences cried out from their dungeons for redress. Some were about to suffer execution without righteousness, others to be sent off to a barbarous country." "The records of justice have been falsified," the pamphlet went on to say, "and the laws profanely altered by men like ourselves. The bloody laws against us have been enforced, under a normal administration, by mere whitened walls, men who possess only the show of justice, and who condemned us to death contrary to law."

That this silly production should be made the subject of a criminal information for libel, rather justifies the belief that an exaggerated importance was given to Lord George's vagaries, both by the Government and his own relations and friends. No doubt he was a thorn in the side of his family, but the ministry could well have afforded to treat him and his utterances with contempt. He was, however, indicted at the King's Bench for publishing the petition, which he had actually himself written, with a view to raise a tumult among the prisoners within Newgate, or cause a disturbance by exciting the compassion of those without.

The case against him was very clearly made out, and as his offence consisted of two parts, Lord George Gordon was subjected to two different sentences. For the first, the publication of the "prisoners' petition," the judge awarded him three years' imprisonment in Newgate. For the second offence, being "trespasses, contempts, and misdemeanours against the royal consort of his most Christian Majesty," the sentence was a fine of £500, with a further imprisonment in Newgate at the termination of the other three; and in addition he was required to give security for fourteen years for his good behaviour, himself in £10,000, and two sureties of £2500 each.

Lord George Gordon remained in Newgate till his death, from gaol-fever, in 1793. He made two or three ineffectual attempts to put in his bail, but they were objected to as insufficient. It was thought to the last that the government and his friends sought pretences to keep him in confinement and out of mischief. His somewhat premature death must have been a relief to them. But it can hardly be denied that hard measure was meted out to him, and if he escaped too easily at his first trial, he was too heavily punished at the second. It is impossible to absolve him from responsibility for the outrages committed by the rioters in 1780, although he was doubtless shocked at their excesses. Lord George could not have foreseen the terrible consequences which would follow his rash agitation, and little knew how dangerous were the elements of disturbance he unchained. But it can hardly be denied that he meant well. Had he lived a century later, he would probably have found a more legitimate outlet for his peculiar tendencies, and would have figured as an ardent philanthropist and platform orator, instead of as a criminal in the dock.

The damages which Newgate sustained at this time were repaired at a cost of about twenty thousand pounds.

CHAPTER III
CELEBRATED CRIMES AND CRIMINALS

State of crime on opening new gaol—Newgate full—Executions very numerous—Ruthless penal code—Forgery punished with death—The first forgery of Bank of England notes—Gibson—Bolland—The two Perreaus—Dr. Dodd—Charles Price, *alias* Old Patch—Clipping still largely practised—John Clarke hanged for it—Also William Guest, a clerk in Bank of England—His elaborate apparatus for filing guineas—Coining—Forty or fifty private mints for making counterfeits—Offences against life and property—Streets unsafe—High roads infested by robbers—No regular police—Daring Robberies at lévees—The Duke of Beaufort robbed by Gentleman Harry—George Barrington, the gentleman thief, frequents Ranelagh, the Palace, the Opera House—Highwaymen put down by the horse patrol—"Long firm" swindlers—Female Sharpers—Elizabeth Grieve and others pretend to sell places under the Crown—Other forms of swindling—Juvenile depravity—A girl for sale—Prize-fighting—Early martyrs to freedom of speech—Prynne, Bastwick and Daniel Defoe—The Press oppressed—The "North Briton"—Wilkes—William Cobbett in Newgate—Also the Marquis of Sligo.

In the years immediately following the erection of the new gaol, crime was once more greatly in the ascendant. After the peace which gave independence to the United States, the country was overrun with discharged soldiers and sailors. The majority were in dire poverty, and took to depredation almost as a matter of course. The calendars were particularly heavy. At this date there were forty-nine persons lying in Newgate under sentence of death, one hundred and eighty under sentence of transportation, and prisoners of other categories, making the total prison population up to nearly six hundred souls.

Speaking of those times, Mr. Townshend, a veteran Bow Street runner, in his evidence before a Parliamentary Committee in 1816, declared that in the years 1781-7 as many as twelve, sixteen, or twenty were hanged at one execution; twice he saw forty hanged at one time. In 1783 there were twenty at two consecutive executions. He had known, he said, as many as two hundred and twenty tried at one sessions. He had himself obtained convictions of from thirteen to twenty-five for returning from transportation. Upon the same authority we are told that in 1783 the Secretary of State advised the King to punish with all severity. The enormity of the offences was so great, says Mr. Townshend, and "plunder had got to such an alarming pitch," that a letter was circulated among judges and recorders then sitting, to the effect that His Majesty would dispense with the recorders' reports, and that the worst criminals should be picked out and at once ordered for execution.

The penal code was at this period still ruthlessly severe in England. There were some two hundred capital felonies upon the statute book. Almost any member of parliament eager to do his share in legislation could "create a capital felony." A story is told of Edmund Burke, that he was leaving his house one day in a hurry, when a messenger called him back on a matter which would not detain him a minute: "Only a felony without benefit of clergy." Burke also told Sir James Mackintosh, that although scarcely entitled to ask a favour of the ministry, he thought he had influence enough to create a capital felony. It is true that of the two hundred, not more than five-and-twenty sorts of felonies actually entailed execution. It is also true that some of the most outrageous and ridiculous reasons for its infliction had disappeared. It was no longer death to take a falcon's egg from the nest, nor was it a hanging matter to be thrice guilty of exporting live sheep. But a man's life was still appraised at five shillings. Stealing from the person, or in a dwelling, or in a shop, or on a navigable river, to that amount, was punished with death. "I think it not right nor justice," wrote Sir Thomas More in 1516, "that the loss of money should cause the loss of man's life; for mine opinion is that all the goods in the world are not able to countervail man's life." Three hundred years was still to pass before the strenuous efforts of Sir Samuel Romilly bore fruit in the amelioration of the penal code. In 1810 he carried a bill through the House of Commons, which was, however, rejected by the Lords, to abolish capital punishment for stealing to the amount of five shillings in a shop. His most bitter opponents were the great lawyers of the times, Lords Ellenborough, Eldon, and others, Lords Chancellors and Lords Chief Justice, who opposed dangerous innovations, and viewed with dismay any attempt "to alter laws which a century had proved to be necessary." Lord Eldon on this occasion said that he was firmly convinced of the wisdom of the principles and practice of the criminal code. Romilly did not live to see the triumph of his philanthropic endeavours. He failed to procure the repeal of the cruel laws against which he raised his voice, but he stopped the hateful legislation which multiplied capital felonies year by year, and his illustrious example found many imitators. Within a few years milder and more humane ideas very generally prevailed. In 1837 the number of offences to which the extreme penalty could be applied was only seven, and in that year only eight persons were executed, all of them for murders of an atrocious character.

Forgery, at the period of which I am now treating, was an offence especially repugnant to the law. No one guilty of it could hope to escape the gallows. The punishment was so certain, that as milder principles gained ground, many benevolent persons gladly withdrew from prosecution where they could. Instances were known in which bankers and other opulent people compromised with the delinquent rather than be responsible for taking away a fellow-creature's life. The prosecutor would sometimes pretend his pockets had been picked of the forged instrument, or he destroyed it, or refused to produce it. An important witness sometimes kept out of the way. Persons have gone so far as to meet forged bills of exchange, and to a large amount. In one case it was pretty certain they would not have advanced the money had the punishment been short of death, because the culprit had already behaved disgracefully, and they had no desire he should escape a lesser retribution. Prosecutors have forfeited their recognizances sooner than appear, and have even, when duly sworn, withheld a portion of their testimony.

But at the time of which I am now writing the law generally took its course. In the years between 1805 and 1818 there had been two hundred and seven executions for forgery; more than for either murder, burglary, or robbery from the person. It may be remarked here that the Bank of England was by far the most bitter and implacable as regards prosecutions for forgery. Of the above-mentioned executions for this crime, no less than seventy-two were the victims of proceedings instituted by the Bank of England. Forgeries upon this great monetary corporation had been much more frequent since the stoppage of specie payments, which had been decreed by the Parliament in 1797 to save the Bank from collapse. Alarms of invasion had produced such a run upon it, that on one particular day little more than a million in cash or bullion remained in the cellars, which had already been drained of specie for foreign subsidies and subventions. Following the cessation of cash payments to redeem its paper in circulation, the Bank had commenced the issue of notes to the value of less than five pounds, and it was soon found that these, especially the one-pound notes, were repeatedly forged. In the eight years preceding 1797 but few prosecutions had been instituted by the Bank; but in the eight years which followed there were one hundred and forty-six convictions for the offence. At last, about 1818, a strong and general feeling of dissatisfaction grew rife against these prosecutions. The crime had continued steadily to increase, in spite of the awful penalties conviction entailed. It was proved, moreover, that note forgery was easily accomplished. Detection, too, was most difficult. The public were unable to distinguish between the good and bad notes. Bank officials were themselves often deceived, and cases were known where the clerks had refused payment of the genuine article. Juries began to decline to convict on the evidence of inspectors and clerks, unless substantiated by the revelation of the private mark, a highly inconvenient practice, which the Bank itself naturally discountenanced. Efforts were made to improve the quality of the note, so as to defy imitation; but this could not well be done at the price, and, as the only effective remedy, specie payments were resumed, and the one-pound note withdrawn from circulation. But execution for forgery continued to be the law for many more years. Fauntleroy suffered for it in 1824; Joseph Hunton, the Quaker linen-draper, in 1828; and Maynard, the last, in the following year.

I am, however, anticipating somewhat, and must retrace my steps, and indicate briefly one or two of the early forgers who passed through Newgate and suffered for the crime. The first case I find recorded is that of Richard Vaughan, a linen-draper of Stafford, who was committed to Newgate in March, 1758, for counterfeiting Bank of England notes. He employed several artists to engrave the notes in various parts, one of whom informed against him. The value of the note he himself added. Twenty which he had thus filled up he had deposited in the hands of a young lady to whom he was paying his addresses, as a guarantee of his wealth. Vaughan no doubt suffered, although I see no record of the fact in the Newgate Calendar.

Mr. Gibson's was a curious case. He was a prisoner in Newgate for eighteen months between conviction and execution, the jury having found a special verdict, subject to the determination of the twelve judges. As Gibson remained so long in gaol, it was the general opinion that no further notice would be taken of the case. The prisoner himself must have been buoyed up with this hope, as he petitioned repeatedly for judgment. He had been sentenced in Sept. 1766, and in 1768, at Hilary Term, the judges decided that his crime came within the meaning of the law. Gibson had been a solicitor's clerk, who gave so much satisfaction that he was taken into partnership. The firm was doing a large business, and among other large affairs was intrusted with a Chancery case, respecting an estate for which an *ad interim* receiver had been appointed. Gibson's way of life was immoral and extravagant. He had urgent need of funds, and in an evil hour he forged the signature of the Accountant-General to the Court of Chancery, and so obtained possession of some of the rents of the above-mentioned estate. The fraud was presently discovered; Gibson was arrested, and eventually, as already stated, condemned. "After sentence," says the Calendar, "his behaviour was in every way becoming his awful situation; ... he appeared rational, serious, and devout. His behaviour was so pious, so resigned, and in all respects so admirably adapted to his unhappy situation, that the tears of the commiserating multitude accompanied his last ejaculation. He was carried to execution in a mourning coach," an especial honour reserved for malefactors of aristocratic antecedents and gentle birth.

James Bolland, who was executed in 1772, deserved and certainly obtained less sympathy. Bolland long filled the post of a sheriff's officer, and as such became the lessee of a spunging-house, where he practised boundless extortion. He was a man of profligate life, whose means never equalled his extravagant self-indulgence, and he was put to all manner of shifts to get money. More than once he arrested debtors, was paid all claims in full, and appropriated the money to his own use, yet escaped due retribution for his fraud. He employed bullies, spies, and indigent attorneys to second his efforts, some of whom were arrested and convicted of other crimes with the clothes Bolland provided for them still on their backs. His character was so infamous, that when he purchased the situation of upper city marshal for £2,400, the court of aldermen would not approve of the appointment. He tried also to succeed to a vacancy as Sergeant-at-mace, and met with the same objection. The deposit-money paid over in both these affairs was attached by his sureties, and he was driven to great necessities for funds. When called upon to redeem a note of hand he had given, he pleaded that he was short of cash, and offered another man's bill, which, however, was refused unless endorsed. Bolland then proceeded to endorse it with his own name, but it was declared unnegotiable, owing to the villainous character he bore. Whereupon Bolland erased all the letters after the capital, and substituted the letters "anks," the name of Banks being that of a respectable victualler of Rathbone Place, in a large way of trade. When the bill became due, Banks repudiated his signature, and Bolland, who sought too late to meet it and hush up the affair, was arrested for the forgery. He was tried and executed in due course.

The case of the twin brothers Perreau in 1776 was long the talk of the town. It evoked much public sympathy, as they were deemed to be the dupes of a certain Mrs. Rudd, who lived with Daniel Perreau, and passed as his wife. Daniel was a man of reputed good means, with a house in Harley Street, which he kept up well. His brother, Robert Perreau, was a surgeon enjoying a large practice, and residing in Golden Square. The forged deed was a bond for £7,500, purporting to be signed by William Adair, a well-known agent. Daniel Perreau handed this to Robert Drummond Perreau, who carried it to the Bank, where its validity was questioned, and the brothers, with Mrs. Rudd, were arrested on suspicion of forgery. Daniel on his trial solemnly declared that he had received the instrument from Mrs. Rudd; Robert's defence was that he had no notion the document was forged. Both were, however, convicted of knowingly uttering the counterfeit bond. It was, however, found impossible to prove Mrs. Rudd's complicity in the transaction, and she was acquitted. The general feeling was, however, so strong that she was the guilty person, that the unfortunate Perreaus became a centre of interest. Strenuous efforts were made to obtain a reprieve for them. Robert Perreau's wife went in deep mourning, accompanied by her three children, to sue on their knees for pardon from the queen. Seventy-two leading bankers and merchants signed a petition in his favour, which was presented to the king two days before the execution: but all to no purpose. Both of the brothers suffered the extreme penalty at Tyburn on the 17th January, 1776, before an enormous multitude estimated at 30,000. They asserted their innocence to the last.

In the following year a clergyman, who had at one time achieved some eminence, also fell a victim to the vindictive laws regarding forgery. Dr. Dodd was the son of a clergyman. He had been a wrangler at Cambridge, and was early known as a litterateur of some repute. While still on his promotion, and leading a gay life in London, he made a foolish marriage, and united himself to the daughter of one of Sir John Dolben's servants, a young lady largely endowed with personal attractions, but certainly deficient in birth and fortune. This sobered him, and he took orders in the year that his "Beauties of Shakespeare" was published. He became a zealous curate at West Ham; thence he went to St. James', Garlick Hill, and took an active part in London church and charitable work. He was one of the promoters of the Magdalen Hospital, also of the Humane Society, and in 1763, twelve years after ordination, he was appointed chaplain in ordinary to the King. About the same time he was presented to a prebend's stall in Brecon Cathedral, and was recommended to Lord Chesterfield as tutor to his son. He hoped to succeed to the rectory of West Ham, but being disappointed he now came to London, and launched out into extravagance. He had a town house, and a country house at Ealing, and he exchanged his chariot for a coach. Having won a prize of £1,000 in a lottery, he became interested in two proprietary chapels, but could not make them pay. But just then he was presented with a living, that of Hockliffe, in Bedfordshire, which he held with the vicarage of Chalgrove, and his means were still ample. They were not sufficient, however, for his expenditure, and in an evil moment he attempted to obtain the valuable cure of St. George's, Hanover Square, by back-stair influence. The living was in the gift of the Crown, and Dodd was so ill-advised as to write to a great lady at Court, offering her £3,000 if he were presented. The letter was forthwith passed on to the Lord Chancellor, and the King, George III, hearing what had happened, ordered Dr. Dodd's name to be struck off the list of his chaplains. The story was made public, and Dodd was satirized in the press and on the stage.

Dodd was now greatly encumbered by debts, from which the presentation to a third living, that of Winge, in Buckinghamshire, could not relieve him. He was in such straits that, according to his biographer, "he descended so low as to become the editor of a newspaper," and he tried to obtain relief in bankruptcy, but failed. At length, so sorely pressed was he by creditors that he resolved to do a dishonest deed. He forged the name of his old pupil, now Lord Chesterfield, who had since become his patron, to a bond for £4,200. He applied to certain usurers, in the name of a young nobleman who was seeking an advance. The business was refused by many, because Dr. Dodd declared that they could not be present at the execution of the bond. A Mr. Robertson proved more obliging, and to him Dr. Dodd, in due course, handed a bond for £4,200 executed by Lord Chesterfield, and witnessed by himself. A second witness being necessary, Mr. Robertson signed his name beneath Dr. Dodd's. The bond was no sooner presented for payment, and referred to Lord Chesterfield, than it was repudiated. Robertson was forthwith arrested, and soon afterwards Dr. Dodd. The latter at once, in the hope of saving himself, returned $3,000; he gave a cheque upon his bankers for £700, a bill of sale on his furniture worth £400 more, and the whole sum was made up by another hundred from the brokers. Nevertheless Dr. Dodd was taken before the Lord Mayor and charged with the forgery. Lord Chesterfield would not stir a finger to help his old tutor, although the poor wretch had made full restitution. Dr. Dodd, when arraigned, declared that he had no intention to defraud, that he had only executed the bond as a temporary resource to meet some pressing claims. The jury after consulting only five minutes found him guilty, and he was regularly sentenced to death. Still greater exertions were made to obtain a reprieve for Dr. Dodd than in the case of the Perreaus. The newspapers were filled with letters pleading for him. All classes of people strove to help him; the parish officers went in mourning from house to house, asking subscriptions to get up a petition to the King, and this petition, when eventually drafted, filled twenty-three skins of parchment. Petitions from Dodd and his wife, both drawn up by Dr. Johnson, were laid before the King and Queen. Even the Lord Mayor and Common Council went in a body to St. James's Palace to beg mercy from the King. As, however, clemency had been denied to the Perreaus, it was deemed unadvisable to extend it to Dr. Dodd. The concourse at his execution, which took place at Tyburn, was immense. It has been stated erroneously that Dr. Dodd preached his own funeral sermon. He only delivered an address to his fellow-prisoners in the prison chapel by the permission of Mr. Villette, the ordinary. The text he chose was Psalm 51:3, "I acknowledge my faults; and my sin is ever before me." It was delivered some three weeks before the Doctor's execution, and subsequently printed. It is a curious fact that among other published works of Dr. Dodd, is a sermon on the injustice of capital punishments. He was, however, himself the chief witness against a highwayman, who was hanged for stopping him. Among other spectators at the execution of Dr. Dodd was the Rev. James Hackman, who afterwards murdered Miss Reay.

It is said that a scheme was devised to procure Dodd's escape from Newgate. He was treated with much consideration by Mr. Akerman, allowed to have books, papers, and a reading-desk. Food and other necessaries were brought him from outside by a female servant daily. This woman was found to bear a striking resemblance to the Doctor, which was the more marked when she was dressed up in a wig and gown. She was asked if she would coöperate in a scheme for taking the Doctor's place in gaol, and consented. It was arranged that on a certain day, Dr. Dodd's irons having been previously filed, he was to change clothes with the woman. She was to seat herself at the reading-desk while Dr. Dodd, carrying a bundle under his arm, coolly walked out of the prison. The plan would probably have succeeded, but Dodd would not be a party to it. He was so buoyed up with the hope of reprieve that he would not risk the misconstruction which would have been placed upon the attempt to escape had it failed. In his own profession Dr. Dodd was not very highly esteemed. Dr. Newton, Bishop of Bristol, is said to have observed that Dodd deserved pity, because he was hanged for the least crime he had committed.

One of the most notorious depredators in this line, whose operations long eluded detection, was Charles Price, commonly called Old Patch. He forged bank-notes wholesale. His plans were laid with the utmost astuteness, and he took extraordinary precautions to avoid discovery. He did everything for himself; made his own paper, with the proper water-mark, engraved his own plates, and manufactured his own ink. His method of negotiating the forged notes was most artful. He had three homes; at one he was Price, properly married, at a second he lived under another name with a woman who helped him in his schemes, at a third he did the actual business of passing his notes. This business was always effected in disguise; none of his agents or instruments saw him except in disguise, and when his work was over he put it off to return home. One favourite personation of his was that of an infirm old man, wearing a long black camlet cloak, with a broad cape fastened up close to his chin. With this he wore a big, broad-brimmed slouch hat, and often green spectacles or a green shade. Sometimes his mouth was covered up with red flannel, or his corpulent legs and gouty feet were swathed in flannel. His natural appearance as Price was a compact middle-aged man, inclined to stoutness, erect, active, and not bad-looking, with a beaky nose, keen gray eyes, and a nutcracker chin. His schemes were very ingenious. On one occasion he pretended, in one disguise, to expose a swindler (himself in another disguise), whom a respectable city merchant inveigled into his house in order to give him up to the police. The swindler proposed to buy himself off for £500; the offer was accepted, the money paid by a thousand-pound note, for which the swindler got change. The note, of course, was forged. He victimized numbers of tradesmen. Disguised as an old man, he passed six forged fifty-pound notes on a grocer, and then as Price backed up his victim in an action brought against the bank which refused payment of the counterfeits. But his cleverest coup was that organized against the lottery offices. Having in one of his disguises engaged a boy to serve him, he sent the lad, dressed in livery, round the town to buy lottery tickets, paying for them in large (forged) notes, for which change was always required. By these means hundreds and hundreds of pounds were obtained upon the counterfeits. The boy was presently arrested, and a clever plot was laid to nab the old man his master, but Price by his vigilance outwitted the police. Another of his dodges was to hire boys to take forged notes to the Bank, receive the tickets from the teller, and carry them back to him. He forthwith altered the figures, passed them on by the same messenger to the Bank cashier, and obtained payment for the larger amount.

These wholesale forgeries produced something like consternation at the Bank. It was supposed that they were executed by a large gang, well organized and with numerous ramifications, although Price, as I have said, really worked single-handed. The notes poured in day after day, and still no clue was obtained as to the culprits. The Bow Street officials were hopelessly at fault. "Old Patch" was advertised for, described in his various garbs. It was now discovered that he had a female accomplice. This was a Mrs. Poultney, alias Hickeringill, his wife's aunt, a tall, rather genteel woman of thirty, with a downcast look, thin face and person, light hair, and pitted with the small-pox. Fate at last unexpectedly overtook Old Patch. One of many endorsements upon a forged note was traced to a pawnbroker, who remembered to have had the note from one Powel. The runners suspected that Powel was Price, and that he was a member of Old Patch's gang. A watch was set at the pawnbroker's, and the next time Powel called he was arrested, identified as Price, searched, and found to have upon his person a large number of notes, with a quantity of white tissue-paper, which he declared he had bought to make into air-balloons for his children. Price was committed to prison, and a close inquiry made into his antecedents. He was found to be the man who had decoyed Foote the actor into a partnership in a brewery and decamped with the profits, leaving Foote to pay liabilities to the extent of £500. Then, he had started an illicit still, and had been arrested and sent to Newgate till he had paid a fine of £1,600. He was released through the intercession of Lord Lyttleton and Foote, and forgiven the fine. He next set up as a fraudulent lottery office keeper, and bolted with a big prize. After this he elaborated his system of forgery, which ended in the way I have said. Price was alert and cunning to the last. One of his first acts was to pass out a clandestine letter to Mrs. Poultney, briefly telling her to destroy everything. This she effected by burning the whole of his disguises in the kitchen fire, on the pretence that the clothes were infected by the plague. The engraving press was disposed of; the copper plates heated red-hot, then smashed into pieces and thrown with the water-mark wires on to a neighbouring dust-heap, where they were subsequently discovered. Price attempted to deny his identity, but to no purpose, and when he saw the grip of the law tightening upon him, he committed suicide to avoid the extreme penalty. He was found hanging behind the door of his cell, suspended from two hat-screws, strengthened by gimlets. Price's depredations, it was said, amounted to £200,000; but how he disposed of his ill-gotten gains, seeing that he always lived obscurely, and neither gambled nor drank, remained an inscrutable secret to the last.

Persons of respectable station, sometimes, succumbed to special temptations. William Guest was the son of a clergyman living at Worcester, who had sufficient interest to get him a clerkship in the Bank of England. The constant handling of piles of gold was too much for Guest's integrity, and he presently resolved to turn his opportunities to account. Taking a house in Broad Street Buildings, he devoted the upper part of it to his nefarious trade. He abstracted guineas from his drawer in the Bank, carried them home, filed them, then remilled them in a machine he had designed for the purpose, and returned them—now light weight—to the Bank. The filings he converted into ingots and disposed of to the trade. No suspicion of his malpractices transpiring, he was in due course advanced to the post of teller. But a fellow-teller having observed him one day picking out new guineas from a bag, watched him, and found that he did this constantly. On another occasion he was seen to pay away guineas some of which, on examination, proved to have been recently filed. They were weighed, and found short weight. To test Mr. Guest still further, his money-bags were opened one night after hours, and the contents counted and examined. The number was short, and several guineas found which appeared to have been recently filed, and which on weighing proved to be light.

A descent was forthwith made upon Guest's house, and in the upper rooms the whole apparatus for filing was laid bare. In a nest of drawers were found vice, files, the milling machine, two bags of gold filings, and a hundred guineas. A flap in front of the nest of drawers could be let down, and inside was a skin fastened to the back of the flap, with a hole in it to button on to the waistcoat, and equip the workman after the method of jewellers. More evidence was soon forthcoming against Guest. His fellow-teller had seen him in possession of a substantial bar of gold; jewellers and others swore to having bought ingots from him, and an assayer at Guest's trial deposed to their being of the same standard as the guinea coinage. His guilt was clearly made out to the jury, and he was sentenced to death. A petition signed by a number of influential persons was forwarded to the Crown, praying for mercy, but it was decided that the law must take its course. As his crime amounted to high treason, he went to Tyburn on a sledge, but he suffered no other penalty than hanging.

The flagitious trade of coining was in a most flourishing condition during the last decades of the eighteenth and the early part of the nineteenth centuries. The condition of the national coinage was at this time far from creditable to the Mint. A great part of both the silver and copper money in circulation was much worn and defaced. Imitation thus became much easier than with coins comparatively fresh and new. Hence the nefarious practice multiplied exceedingly. There were as many as forty or fifty private mints constantly at work, either in London or in the principal country towns. The process was rapid, not too laborious, and extremely profitable. A couple of hands could turn out in a week base silver coins worth nominally two or three hundred pounds. The wages of a good workman were as much as a couple of guineas a day. Much capital was invested by large dealers in the trade, who must have made enormous sums. One admitted that his transactions in seven years amounted to the production of £200,000 in counterfeit half-crowns and other silver coins. So systematic was the traffic, that orders for town and country were regularly executed by the various manufacturers. Boxes and parcels of base coin were despatched every morning by coach and wagon to all parts of the kingdom, like any other goods. The trade extended to foreign countries. The law, until it was rectified, did not provide any method of punishment for the counterfeiting of foreign money, and French louis-d'or, Spanish dollars, German florins, and Turkish sequins were shipped abroad in great quantities. The Indian possessions even did not escape, and a manufactory of spurious gold or silver pagodas was at one time most active in London, whence they were exported to the East. The number of persons employed in London as capitalists and agents for distribution alone amounted to one hundred and twenty at one time; and besides there was a strong force of skilful handicraftsmen, backed up by a whole army of "utterers" or "smashers," constantly busy in passing the base money into the currency. The latter comprised hawkers, peddlers, market-women, hackney-coach drivers, all of whom attended the markets held by the dealers in the manufactured article, and bought wholesale to distribute retail by various devices, more particularly in giving change. They obtained the goods at an advantage of about one hundred per cent. When the base money lost its veneer, the dealers were ready to repurchase it in gross, and after a repetition of the treatment, issue it afresh at the old rates.

Gold coins were not so much counterfeited as silver and copper, but there were many bad guineas in circulation. The most dexterous method of coining them was by mixing a certain amount of alloy with the pure metal. They were the proper weight, and had some semblance of the true ring, but their intrinsic value was not more than thirteen or fourteen shillings, perhaps only eight or nine. The fabrication was, however, limited by the expense and the nicety required in the process. To counterfeit silver was a simpler operation. Of base silver money there were five kinds; viz., flats, plated goods, plain goods, castings, and "fig" things. The *flats* were cut out of prepared flattened plates composed of silver and blanched copper. When cut out the coins were turned in a lathe, stamped in a press with the proper die, and subjected to rubbing with various materials, including aquafortis to bring the silver to the surface, sand-paper, cork, cream of tartar, and last of all blacking to give the appearance of age. *Plated goods* were prepared from copper; the coins cut the proper size and plated, the stamping being done afterwards. As these coins were very like silver, they generally evaded detection. *Plain goods* consisted of copper blanks the size of a shilling, turned out from a lathe, then given the colour and lustre of metal buttons, after which they were rubbed with cream of tartar and blacking. *Castings*, as the word implies, were coins made of blanched copper, cast in moulds of the proper die; they were then silvered and treated like the rest. It was very common to give this class of base money a crooked appearance, by which means they seemed genuine, and got into circulation without suspicion. The "*figs*" or *fig things*, were the lowest and meanest class, and were confined chiefly to sixpences. Copper counterfeit money was principally of two kinds, stamped and plain, made out of base metal; the profit on them being about a hundred per cent. They were mostly halfpennies; but farthings were also largely manufactured, the material being real copper, but the fraud consisted in their being of light weight, and very thin.

The prosecutions for coining were very numerous. The register of the solicitor to the Mint recorded as many as six hundred and fifty in a period of seven years. The offence of uttering, till a recent date, constituted petty treason, and met with the usual penalties. These, in the case of female offenders, included hanging and burning at a stake. The last woman who suffered in this way was burned before the debtors' door, in front of Newgate, in 1788, having previously been strangled. In the following year, as has been already stated, the law was passed, which abolished the practice of burning women convicted of petty treason, and thereafter persons guilty of only selling or dealing in base money were more leniently dealt with. The offence was long only a misdemeanour, carrying with it a sentence of imprisonment for a year and a day, which the culprit passed not unpleasantly in Newgate, while his friends or relations kept the business going outside, and supplied him regularly with ample funds.

There was as yet little security for life and property in town or country. The streets of London were still unsafe; high roads and bye roads leading to it were still infested by highway robbers. The protection afforded to the public by the police continued very inefficient. It was still limited to parochial effort; the watchmen were appointed by the vestries, and received a bare pittance,— twelve and sixpence a week in summer, seventeen and sixpence in winter,— which they often eked out by taking bribes from the women of the town, or by a share in a burglar's "swag," to whose doings they were conveniently blind. These watchmen were generally middle-aged, often old and feeble men, who were appointed either from charitable motives, to give them employment, or save them from being inmates of the workhouse and a burthen to the parish. Their hours of duty were long, from night-fall to sunrise, during which, when so disposed, they patrolled the streets, calling the hour, the only check on their vigilance being the occasional rounds of the parish beadle, who visited the watchmen on their various beats. In spite of this the watchmen were often invisible; not to be found when most wanted, and even when present, powerless to arrest or make head against disorderly or evilly-disposed persons.

Besides the watchmen there were the parish constables, nominated by the court of burgesses, or court leet. The obligation of serving in the office of constable might fall upon any householder in turn, but he was at liberty to escape it by buying a substitute or purchasing a "Tyburn ticket," exempting from service. The parish constables were concerned with pursuit rather than prevention, with crime after rather than before the fact. In this duty they were assisted by the police constables, although there was no love lost between the two classes of officer. The police constables are most familiar to us under the name of "Bow Street runners," but they were attached to all the police offices, and not to Bow Street alone. They were nominated from Whitehall by the Secretary of State, the minister now best known as the Home Secretary. The duties of the "runners" were mainly those of detection and pursuit, in which they were engaged in London and in the country, at home and abroad. Individuals or public bodies applied to Bow Street, or some other office, for the services of a runner. These officers took charge of poaching cases, of murders, burglaries, or highway robberies. Some were constantly on duty at the court, as depredations were frequently committed in the royal palaces, or the royal family were "teased by lunatics." The runners were remunerated by a regular salary of a guinea a week; but special services might be recognized by a share in the private reward offered, or, in case of conviction, by a portion of the public parliamentary reward of £40, which might be granted by the bench.

Thieving Lane
(*View of southern end of Thieving Lane, now Bow Street*)

Felons were conveyed through this lane to the gate-house which stood at the end of Tothill Street. In close proximity to the prison, it was a resort of thieves, from which it took its unenviable name.

The policy of making these grants was considered questionable. It tended to tempt officers of justice "to forswear themselves for the lucre of the reward," and the thirst for "blood-money," as it was called, was aggravated till it led many to sell the lives of their fellow-creatures for gain. There were numerous cases of this. Jonathan Wild was one of the most notorious of the dishonest thief-takers. In 1755 several scoundrels of the same ilk were convicted of having obtained the conviction of innocent people, simply to pocket the reward. Their offence did not come under penal statute, so they were merely exposed in the pillory, where, however, the mob pelted one to death and nearly killed another. Again, in 1816, a police officer named Vaughan was guilty of inciting to crime, in order to betray his victims and receive the blood-money. On the other hand, when conviction was doubtful the offender enjoyed long immunity from arrest. Officers would not arrest him until he "weighed his weight," as the saying was, or until they were certain of securing the £40 reward. Another form of remuneration was the bestowal on conviction of a "Tyburn ticket;" in other words, of an exemption from service in parish offices. This the officer sold for what it would bring, the price varying in different parishes from £12 to £40.

It was not to be wondered at that a weak and inadequate police force, backed up by such uncertain and injudicious incentives to activity, should generally come off second-best in its struggles with the hydra-headed criminality of the day. Robberies and burglaries were committed almost under the eyes of the police. It was calculated that the value of the property stolen in the city in one month of 1808 amounted to £15,000, and none of the parties were ever known or apprehended, although sought after night and day. Such cases as the following were of frequent occurrence: "Seven ruffians, about eight o'clock at night knocked at the door of Mrs. Abercrombie in Charlotte Street, Rathbone Place, calling out 'Post!' and upon its being opened, rushed in and took her jewels and fifty or sixty guineas in money, with all the clothes and linen they could get. The neighbourhood was alarmed, and a great crowd assembled, but the robbers sallied forth, and with swords drawn and pistols presented, threatened destruction to any who opposed them. The mob tamely suffered them to escape with their booty without making any resistance." The officers of justice were openly defied. There were streets, such as Duck Lane, Gravel Lane, or Cock Lane, in which it was unsafe for any one to venture without an escort of five or six of his fellows, as the ruffians would cut him to pieces if he were alone.

Still more dastardly were the wanton outrages perpetrated upon unprotected females, often in broad daylight, and in the public streets. These at one time increased to an alarming extent. Ladies were attacked and wounded without warning, and apparently without cause. The injuries were often most serious. On one occasion a young lady was stabbed in the face by means of an instrument concealed in a bouquet of flowers which a ruffian had begged her to smell. When consternation was greatest, however, it was reported that the cowardly assailant was in custody. He proved to be one Renwick Williams, now generally remembered as "the monster." The assault for which he was arrested was made in St. James's Street, about midnight, upon a young lady, Miss Porter, who was returning from a ball to her father's house. Renwick struck at her with a knife, and wounded her badly through her clothes, accompanying the blow with the grossest language. The villain at the time escaped, but Miss Porter recognized him six months later in St. James's Park. He was followed by a Mr. Coleman to his quarters at No. 52, Jermyn Street, and brought to Miss Porter's house. The young lady, crying "That is the wretch!" fainted away at the sight of him. The prisoner indignantly repudiated that he was "the monster" who was advertised for, but he was indicted at the Old Bailey, and the jury found him guilty without hesitation. His sentence was two years' imprisonment in Newgate, and he was bound over in £400 to be of good behaviour.

Gentlemen, some of the highest station, going or returning from court, were often the victims of the depredations committed in the royal precincts. In 1792 a gang of thieves dressed in court suits smuggled themselves into a drawing-room of St. James's Palace, and tried to hustle and rob the Prince of Wales. The Duke of Beaufort, returning from a levee, had his "George," pendant to his ribbon of the Garter, stolen from him in the yard of St. James's Palace. The order was set with brilliants, worth a very large sum of money. The duke called out to his servants, who came up and seized a gentlemanly man dressed in black standing near. The "George" was found in this gentleman's pocket. He proved to be one Henry Sterne, commonly called Gentleman Harry,[82:1] who, being of good address and genteel appearance, easily got admission to the best company, upon whom he levied his contributions.

George Barrington, the notorious pickpocket, also found it to his advantage to attend levees and drawing-rooms. Barrington, or Waldron, which was his real name, began crime early. When one of a strolling company in Ireland, he recruited the empty theatrical treasury and supplemented meagre receipts by stealing watches and purses, the proceeds being divided among the rest of the actors. He found thieving so much more profitable than acting that he abandoned the latter in favour of the former profession, and set up as a gentleman pickpocket. Having worked Dublin well, his native land became too hot to hold him, and he came to London. At Ranelagh one night he relieved both the Duke of Leinster and Sir William Draper of considerable sums. He visited also the principal watering places, including Bath, but London was his favourite hunting-ground. Disguised as a clergyman, he went to court on drawing-room days, and picked pockets or removed stars and decorations from the breasts of their wearers. At Covent Garden Theatre one night he stole a gold snuff-box set with brilliants, and worth £30,000, belonging to Prince Orloff, of which there had been much talk, and which, with other celebrated jewels, Barrington had long coveted. The Russian prince felt the thief's hand in his pocket, and immediately seized Barrington by the throat, on which the latter slipped back the snuff-box. But Barrington was arrested and committed for trial, escaping this time because Prince Orloff would not prosecute. He was, however, again arrested for picking a pocket in Drury Lane Theatre, and sentenced to three years' hard labour on board the hulks in the Thames.

From this he was released prematurely through the good offices of a gentleman who pitied him, only to be reimprisoned, but in Newgate, not the hulks, for fresh robberies at the Opera House, Pantheon, and other places of public resort. Once more released, he betook himself to his old evil courses, and having narrowly escaped capture in London, wandered through the northern counties in various disguises, till he was at length taken at Newcastle-on-Tyne. Another narrow escape followed, through the absence of a material witness; but he was finally arrested for picking a pocket on Epsom Downs, and sentenced to seven years' transportation. He made an affecting speech at his trial, urging, in extenuation of his offence, that he had never had a fair chance of earning an honest livelihood. He may have been sincere, and he certainly took the first opportunity offered to prove it. On the voyage out to New South Wales there was a mutiny on board the convict ship, which would have been successful but for Barrington's aid on the side of authority. He held the passage to the quarter-deck single-handed, and kept the mob of convicts at bay with a marline-spike, till the captain and crew were able to get arms and finally suppress the revolt. As a reward for his conduct, Barrington was appointed to a position of trust, in charge of other prisoners at Paramatta. Within a year or two he was advanced to the more onerous and responsible post of chief constable, and was complimented by the governor of the colony for his faithful performance of the duty. He fell away in health, however, and retiring eventually upon a small pension, died before he was fifty years of age.

The gentlemen of the highway continued to harass and rob all travellers. All the roads were infested. Two or three would be heard of every morning; some on Hounslow Heath, some on Finchley Common, some on Wimbledon Common, some on the Romford Road. Townshend, the Bow Street runner, declared that on arriving at the office of a morning people came in one after the other to give information of such robberies. "Messrs. Mellish, Bosanquet, and Pole, merchants of the city," says a contemporary chronicle, "were stopped by three highwaymen on Hounslow Heath. After robbing them, without resistance, of their money and their watches, one of the robbers wantonly fired into the chaise and mortally wounded Mr. Mellish." The first successful effort made to put down this levying of blackmail upon the king's highway was the establishment of the police horse patrol in 1805. It was organized by the direction of the chief magistrate at Bow Street, then Sir Nathaniel Conant, and under the immediate orders of a conductor, Mr. Day. This force consisted of mounted constables, who every night regularly patrolled all the roads leading into the metropolis. They worked singly between two stations, each starting at a fixed time from each end, halting midway to communicate, then returning. The patrol acted on any information received *en route*, making themselves known as they rode along to all persons riding horses or in carriages, by calling out in a loud tone "Bow Street Patrol." They arrested all known offenders whom they met with, and were fully armed for their own and the public protection. The members of this excellent force were paid eight-and-twenty shillings a week, with turnpike tolls and forage for their horses, which, however, they were obliged to groom and take care of. Marked and immediate results were obtained from the establishment of this patrol. Highway robbery ceased almost entirely, and in the rare cases which occurred before it quite died out, the guilty parties were invariably apprehended.

There was as yet no very marked diminution in the number of executions, but other forms of punishment were growing into favour. Already transportation beyond the seas had become a fixed system. Since the settlement of New South Wales as a penal colony in 1780, convicts were sent out regularly, and in increasingly large batches. The period between conviction and embarkation was spent in Newgate, thus adding largely to its criminal population, with disastrous consequences to the health and convenience of the place. Besides these, the most heinous criminals, there were other lesser offenders, for whom various terms of imprisonment was deemed a proper and sufficient penalty. Hence gaols were growing much more crowded, and Newgate more especially, as will presently be apparent from a brief review of some of the types of persons who became lodgers in Newgate, not temporarily, as in the case of all who passed quickly from the condemned cells to the gallows, but who remained there for longer periods, whether awaiting removal as transports, or working out a sentence of imprisonment in the course of law.

As London, increasing in size and life, became more complex, chances multiplied for rogues and sharpers, who tried with chicane and stratagem to prey upon society. Swindling was carried out more systematically and upon a wider scale than in the days of Jenny Diver or the sham German Princess. A woman named Robinson was arrested in 1801, who, under the pretence of being a rich heiress, had obtained goods fraudulently from tradesmen to the value of £20,000. Again, some years later, a gang resembling somewhat the "long firms" of modern days carried on a fictitious trade, and obtained goods from city merchants worth £50,000. There were many varieties of the professional swindler in those days. Some did business under the guise of licensed and outwardly respectable pawnbrokers, who *sub rosâ* were traffickers in stolen goods. Others roamed the country as hawkers, general dealers, and peddlers, distributing exciseable articles which had been smuggled into the country, carrying on fraudulent raffles, purchasing stolen horses in one county and disposing of them in another. The "duffer" went from door to door in the town, offering for sale smuggled tobacco, muslins, or other stuffs, and, if occasion served, passing forged notes or bad money as small change.

Where the swindler possessed such qualifications as a pleasing manner and a gentlemanly address, with a small capital to start with, he flew at higher game. Alexander Day, alias Marmaduke Davenport, Esq., was one of the first of a long line of impostors who made a great show, in a fine house in a fashionable neighbourhood, with sham footmen in smart liveries, and a grand carriage and pair. The latter he got in on approval, taking care while he used them to be driven to the Duke of Montague's and other aristocratic mansions. In the carriage too he called on numbers of tradesmen and gave large orders for goods: yards of Spanish point-lace, a gold "equipage" or dinner-service, silks in long pieces, table and other linen enough to furnish several houses. By clever excuses he postponed payment, or made off with the property by a second door. Among other things ordered was a gold chain for his squirrel, which already wore a silver one. The goldsmith recognized the silver chain as one he had recently sold to a lady, and his suspicions were aroused. On reference to her she denounced Day as a swindler, who had cheated her out of a large sum of money. Day was forthwith arrested and sent to Newgate. At his trial he declared that he meant to pay for everything he had ordered, that he owned an estate in Durham worth £1,200 a year, but that it was heavily mortgaged. The case occupied some time, but in the end Day was sentenced to two years' imprisonment in Newgate, to stand twice in the pillory, find security for his good behaviour, and pay a fine of £200.

The cleverest swindles were often effected by the softer sex. Female sharpers infested all places of public resort. They dressed in the best clothes, and personating ladies of the highest fashion, attended entertainments and masquerades; they even succeeded in gaining admission to St. James's Palace, where they got into the general circle and pilfered right and left. One woman, the wife of a notorious Chevalier d'Industrie, was known to have been at court at the birthday of King George III. Her costume was in irreproachably good taste; her husband attended her in the garb of a dignitary of the Church. Between them they managed to levy contributions to the extent of £1,700, and made off before these thefts were discovered or suspected.

A notable female sharper was Elizabeth Harriet Grieve, whose line of business was to pretend that she possessed great influence at court, and promise preferment. She gave out that she was highly connected: Lord North was her first cousin, the Duke of Grafton her second; she was nearly related to Lady Fitz-Roy, and most intimate with Lord Guildford and other peers. In those days places were shamelessly bought and sold, and tradesmen retiring from business, or others who had amassed a little property, invested their savings in a situation under the Crown. When the law at length laid hands on the "Hon." Elizabeth Harriet, as she styled herself, a great number of cases were brought against her. A coach-carver, whose trade was declining, had paid her £36 to obtain him a place as clerk in the Victualling Office. Another man gave her £30 down, with a conditional bond for £250, to get the place of a "coast" or "tide"-waiter. Both were defrauded. There were many more proved against her, and she was eventually sentenced to transportation.

She was only one of many who followed the same trade. David James Dignum was convicted in 1777 of pretending to sell places under Government, and sentenced to hard labour on the Thames. Dignum's was a barefaced kind of imposition. He went the length of handing his victims, in exchange for the fees, which were never less than a hundred guineas, a stamped parchment duly signed by the head of the public department, with seals properly attached. In one case he got £1,000 for pretending to secure a person the office of "writer of the 'London Gazette.'" Of course the signatures to these instruments were forged, and the seals had been removed from some legal warrant. When the time came for Dignum's departure for the hulks, he resolved to go to Woolwich in state, and travelled down in a post-chaise, accompanied by his negro servant. But on reaching the ballast lighter on which Dignum was to work, his valet was refused admittance, and the convict was at once put to the duty of the wheelbarrow. He made a desperate effort to get off by forging a cheque on Drummonds, which he got others to cash. They were arrested, but their innocence was clearly shown. Dignum had hoped to be brought up to London for examination. He had thought to change his lot, to exchange the hulks for Newgate, even at the risk of winding up at Tyburn. But in this he was foiled, as the authorities thought it best to institute no prosecution, but leave him to work out his time at the hulks.

That the dishonest and evilly-disposed should thus try to turn the malversation of public patronage to their own advantage was not strange. The traffic in places long flourished unchecked in a corrupt age, and almost under the very eyes of careless, not to say culpable, administrators. The evil practice culminated in the now nearly forgotten case of Mrs. Mary Ann Clarke, who undoubtedly profited liberally by her pernicious influence over the Duke of York when commander-in-chief of the army. The scandal was brought prominently before the public by Colonel Wardle, M. P., who charged her with carrying on a traffic in military commissions, not only with the knowledge, but the participation, of the Duke of York. A long inquiry followed, at which extraordinary disclosures were made. Mrs. Clarke was proved to have disposed of both military and ecclesiastical patronage. She gave her own footman a pair of colours, and procured for an Irish clergyman the honour of preaching before the King. Her brokership extended to any department of state, and her lists of applicants included numbers of persons in the best classes of society. The Duke of York was exonerated from the charge of deriving any pecuniary benefit from this disgraceful traffic; but it was clear that he was cognizant of Mrs. Clarke's proceedings, and that he knowingly permitted her to barter his patronage for filthy lucre. Mrs. Clarke was examined in person at the bar of the house. In the end a vote acquitted the duke of personal corruption, and the matter was allowed to drop. But a little later Colonel Wardle was sued by an upholsterer for furniture supplied at his order to Mrs. Clarke, and the disinterestedness of the colonel's exposure began to be questioned. In 1814 Mrs. Clarke was sentenced to nine months' imprisonment for a libel on the Irish Chancellor of the Exchequer.

A clever scheme of deception which went very near success was that perpetrated by Robert Jaques. Jaques filled the post of "clerk of the papers" to the warden of the Fleet, a place which he had himself solicited, on the plea that he was a man of experience, able to guard the warden against the tricks incident to his trust. Jaques admitted that his own antecedents were none of the best, that he had been frequently in gaol, but he pleaded that men like himself, who had been guilty of the worst offences, had afterwards become the best officers. No sooner was Jaques appointed than he began to mature a plot against his employer. The warden of the Fleet by his office became responsible for the debt of any prisoner in his custody who might escape. Jaques at once cast about for some one whom he might through a third party cause to be arrested, brought to the Fleet on a sham action, and whom he would assist to escape. The third party's business would then be to sue the warden for the amount of the evaded debt. Jaques applied to a friend, Mr. Tronson, who had been a servant, an apothecary, a perfumer, and a quack doctor. Tronson found him one Shanley, a needy Irishman, short of stature and of fair complexion, altogether a person who might well be disguised as a woman. Jaques next arranged that a friend should get a warrant against Shanley for £450. Upon this, Shanley, who was easily found, being a dressy young gentleman, fond of blue and gold, was arrested and carried to a spunging-house. While there a second writ was served upon Shanley for £850, at the suit of another friend of Jaques. Shanley was next transferred to the Fleet on a Habeas, applied for by a fictitious attorney. The very next Sunday, Jaques gave a dinner-party, at which his wife, a brother, Mr. John Jaques, and his wife, with some of the parties to the suits, and of course Shanley, were present. Later in the day Shanley exchanged clothes with Mrs. John Jaques, and, personating her, walked out of the prison. It was at a time when an under-turnkey was on duty at the gate, and he let the disguised prisoner pass without question. By-and-by Mrs. Jaques got back her clothes, and also left. Shanley had meanwhile proceeded post haste to Dover, and so reached the continent.

As soon as the escape was discovered, suspicion fell on Jaques's friends, who were openly taxed with connivance. The matter looked worse for them when they laid claim to the money considered forfeited by the disappearance of the debtor, and the law stepped in to prosecute inquiry. The head turnkey, tracking Shanley to Calais, went in pursuit. At the same time a correspondence which was in progress between the conspirators on either side of the Channel was intercepted by order of the Secretary of State, and the letters handed over to the warden's solicitors. From these the whole plot was discovered, and the guilt of the parties rendered the more sure by the confession of Shanley. Jaques was arrested, tried, and convicted at the Old Bailey, receiving the sentence of three years' imprisonment, with one public exposure on the pillory at the Royal Exchange. A curious accident, however, helped to obtain the premature release of Jaques from Newgate. A Sir James Saunderson having been robbed of a large sum in cash and notes, portion of the stolen property was brought into Newgate by some of the thieves, who were arrested on another charge. The notes were intrusted to Jaques, who pretended he could raise money on them. Instead of this, he gave immediate notice to their rightful owner that he had them in his possession. Jaques afterwards petitioned Sir James Saunderson to interest himself in his behalf, and through this gentleman's good offices he escaped the exposure upon the pillory, and was eventually pardoned.

A peculiar feature in the criminal records of the early part of the last century was the general increase in juvenile depravity. This was remarked and commented upon by all concerned in the administration of justice: magistrates of all categories, police officers, gaolers, and philanthropists. It was borne out, moreover, by the statistics of the times. There were in the various London prisons, in the year 1816, three thousand inmates under twenty years of age. Nearly half of this number were under seventeen, and a thousand of these alone were convicted of felony. Many of those sent to prison were indeed of tender years. Some were barely nine or ten. Children began to steal when they could scarcely crawl. Cases were known of infants of barely six charged in the courts with crimes. This deplorable depravity was attributable to various causes: to the profligacy prevailing in the parish schools; the cruel and culpable neglect of parents who deserted their offspring, leaving them in a state of utter destitution, or were guilty of the no less disgraceful wickedness of using them as instruments for their nefarious designs; the artfulness of astute villains—prototypes of old Fagin—who trained the youthful idea, in their own devious ways. The last-named was a fruitful source of juvenile crime. Children were long permitted to commit small thefts with impunity. The offence would have been death to those who used them as catspaws; for them capital punishment was humanely nearly impossible; moreover, the police officers ignored them till they "weighed their weight," or had been guilty of a forty-pound crime. The education in iniquity continued steadily. They went from bad to worse, and ere long became regular inmates of "flash houses," where both sexes mixed freely with vicious companions of their own age, and the most daring enjoyed the hero-worship of their fellows. When thus assembled, they formed themselves into distinct parties or gangs, each choosing one of their number as captain, and dividing themselves into reliefs to work certain districts, one by day and by night. When they had "collared their swag," they returned to divide their plunder, having gained sometimes as much as three or four hundred pounds. A list, prepared about this date, of these horrible dens showed that there were two hundred of them, frequented by six thousand boys and girls, who lived solely in this way, or were the associates of thieves. These haunts were situated in St. Giles, Drury Lane, Chick Lane, Saffron Hill, the Borough, and Ratcliffe Highway. Others that were out of luck crowded the booths of Covent Garden, where all slept promiscuously amongst the rotting garbage of the stalls. During the daytime all were either actively engaged in thieving, or were revelling in low amusements. Gambling was a passion with them, indulged in without let or hindrance in the open streets; and from tossing buttons there they passed on to playing in the low publics at such games as "put," or "the rocks of Scylla," "bumble puppy," "tumble tumble," or "nine holes."

Still more demoralizing than the foregoing was the pernicious habit, commonly, but happily not invariably followed, of committing these young thieves to Newgate. Here these tyros were at once associated with the veterans and great leaders in crime. Old house-breakers expatiated upon their own deeds, and found eager and willing pupils among their youthful listeners. The elder and more evilly experienced boys soon debased and corrupted their juniors. One with twenty previous convictions against him, who had been in Newgate as often, would have alongside him an infant of seven or eight, sent to gaol for the first time for stealing a hearth-broom. It was as bad or worse for the females. Girls of twelve or thirteen were mixed up with the full-grown felons—women who were what would be styled to-day habitual criminals, as in the well-known case of one who had been committed thirty times to Newgate, residing there generally nine months out of every twelve, and who was the wardswoman or prisoner-officer, with nearly unlimited power.

The crying evils of the system had moved private philanthropy to do something remedial. Charitable schools were started,—the forerunners of our modern reformatories, and the nuclei of time-honoured institutions still flourishing, and worthy of all praise. Other well-meaning people, each with his own pet scheme, began to theorize and propose the construction of juvenile penitentiaries, economical imitations mostly of the great penitentiary which was now nearly completed at Millbank. But juvenile crime still grew and flourished, the offences were as numerous as ever, and their character was mostly the same. The favourite pastime was that of picking pockets. Boys then as now were especially skilful at this in a crowd; short, active little chaps, they slipped through quickly with their booty, and passed it on to the master who was directing the operations. Shop-lifting, again, was much practised, the dodge being to creep along on hands and feet to the shop fronts of haberdashers and linen-drapers, and snatch what they could. Again, there were clever young thieves who could "starr" a pane in a window, and so get their hands through the glass. There were also boys convicted of highway robbery, like Joseph Wood and Thomas Underwood, one fourteen and the other twelve, both of whom were hanged. Another boy, barely sixteen, was executed for setting his master's house on fire. The young incendiary was potboy at a public-house, and having been reprimanded for neglect, vowed revenge. Another boy was condemned for forming one of a gang of boys and girls in a street robbery, who fell upon a man in liquor. The girls attacked him, and the boys stripped him of all he had.

Perhaps the most astounding precocity in crime was that displayed by a boy named Leary, who was tried and sentenced to death at thirteen years of age for stealing a watch and chain from some chambers in the Temple. He began at the early age of eight, and progressed regularly from stealing apples to burglary and household robbery. He learned the trade first from a companion at school. After exacting toll from the tart-shops, he took to stealing bakers' loaves, then money from shop-counters and tills, or breaking shop-windows and drawing their contents through. He often appeared at school with several pounds in his pocket, the proceeds of his depredations. He soon became captain of a gang known as Leary's gang, who drove about, armed with pistols, in a cart, watching for carriages with the trunks fastened outside, which they could cut away. In these excursions the gang was often out for a week or more, Leary's share of the profits amounting sometimes to £100. Once, as the result of several robberies in and about London, he amassed some £350, but the money was partly stolen from him by older thieves, or he squandered it in gambling, or in the flash houses. After committing innumerable depredations, he was captured in a gentleman's dining-room in the act of abstracting a quantity of plate. He was found guilty, but out of compassion committed to the Philanthropic School, but escaped, was again caught, and eventually sentenced to transportation for life.

The prevailing tastes of the populace were in these times low and depraved. Their amusements were brutal, their manners and customs disreputable, their morality at the lowest ebb. It is actually on record that little more than a hundred years ago a man and his wife were convicted of offering their niece, "a fine young girl, apparently fourteen years of age," for sale at the Royal Exchange. Mr. and Mrs. Crouch were residents of Bodmin, Cornwall, to which remote spot came a report that maidens were very scarce in London, and that they sold there for a good price. They accordingly travelled up to town by road, two hundred and thirty-two miles, and on arrival hawked the poor girl about the streets. At length they "accosted an honest captain of a ship, who instantly made known the base proposal they had made to him." The Crouches were arrested and tried; the man was sentenced to six months' imprisonment in Newgate, but his wife, as having acted under his influence, was acquitted.

Traffic in dead bodies was more actively prosecuted. The wretches who gained the name of Resurrection men despoiled graveyards to purvey subjects for the dissecting knife. There were dealers who traded openly in these terrible goods, and, as has been previously described, their agents haggled for corpses at the foot of the gallows. Sometimes the culprits were themselves the guardians of the sacred precincts. I find that the grave-digger of St. George's, Bloomsbury, was convicted, with a female accomplice, of stealing a dead body, and sentenced to imprisonment. They were also "whipped twice on their bare backs from the end of King's Gate Street, Holborn, to Dyot Street, St. Giles, being half a mile." There was a great development of this crime later in the persons of Burke and Hare.

Disorderly gatherings for the prosecution of the popular sports were of constant occurrence. The vice of gambling was openly practised in the streets. It was also greatly fostered by the metropolitan fairs, of which there were eighty annually, lasting from Easter to September, when Bartholomew Fair was held. These fairs were the resort of the idle and the profligate, and most of the desperate characters in London were included in the crowd. Another favourite amusement was bull-baiting or bullock-hunting. Sunday morning was generally chosen for this pastime. A subscription was made to pay the hire of an animal from some drover or butcher, which was forthwith driven through the most populous parts of the town; often across church-yards when divine service was in progress, pursued by a yelling mob, who goaded the poor brute to madness with sharp pointed sticks, or thrust peas into its ears. When nearly dead the poor beast rejoined its herd, and was driven on to Smithfield market. A system of bull-baits was introduced at Westminster by two notorious characters known as Caleb Baldwin and Hubbersfield, otherwise Slender Billy, which attracted great crowds, and led to drunkenness and scenes of great disorder.

Towards the close of the eighteenth century a still lower and more debasing amusement sprang suddenly into widespread popularity. The patronage of pugilism or prize-fighting was no doubt supposed by many to be the glorification of the national virtues of courage and endurance. It was also greatly due to the gradual disuse of the practice of carrying side-arms, when it was thought that quarrels would be fought out with fists instead of swords. Hence the "noble art of self-defence," as it was styled magniloquently, found supporters in every class of society. Prize-fights first became fashionable about 1788, following a great encounter between two noted pugilists, named Richard Humphreys and Daniel Mendoza, a Jew. Sporting papers were filled with accounts of the various fights, which peer and pickpocket attended side by side, and which even a Royal Prince did not disdain to honour. These professional bruisers owned many noble patrons. Besides, the Prince of Wales, the Dukes of Clarence and York, the Duke of Hamilton, Lords Barrymore and others, attended prize-fights and sparring matches at theatres and public places. A well-known pugilist, who was summoned for an assault at Covent Garden Theatre, brought forward in his defence his intimacy with a number of noted people; the very day on which he was charged, he pleaded that he had dined at the Piazza Coffee House with General Gwynne, Colonel McDouel, Captains Barkley and Hanbury, after which they had all gone to the theatre. These aristocratic friends were, moreover, ready to be useful at a pinch, and would bail out a pugilist in trouble, or give him their countenance and support. At the trial of one William Ward, who had killed a man in a fight, the pugilist was attended by his patrons in court. The case was a bad one. Ward, on his way to see a fight in the country, had been challenged by a drunken blacksmith, and proved to him after a few rounds that he was no match for the trained bruiser. The blacksmith did not like his "punishment," and tried to escape into the bar, when his antagonist followed him, and actually beat him to death. At the trial Ward was found guilty of manslaughter, fined one shilling, and only sentenced to be imprisoned three months in Newgate. Yet the judge who inflicted this light punishment condemned boxing as an inhuman and disgraceful practice, a disgrace to any civilized nation.

To the foregoing categories of undoubted criminals must be added another somewhat numerous class of offenders, who were so deemed by the contemporary codes, and who now frequently found themselves relegated to Newgate. These were days when the press had far from achieved its present independence; when writers, chafing under restraints and reckless of consequence, were tempted into license from sheer bravado and opposition; when others far more innocent were brought under the same ban of the law, and suffered imprisonment and fine for a hardly unwarrantable freedom of speech. It is to be feared that the frequent prosecutions instituted had often their origin in political antipathy. While ministerial prints might libel and revile the opponents of the governments, journals which did not spare the party in power were humiliated and brow-beaten, difficulties were thrown in the way of their obtaining intelligence, and if they dared to express their opinions freely, "an information *ex officio*," as it was styled, was issued by the Attorney-General. Prosecution followed, protracted to the bitter end. Even what seems to us the harmless practice of parliamentary reporting was deemed a breach of privilege; it was tolerated, but never expressly permitted. Offending journalists were often reprimanded at the bar of the House, and any member who felt aggrieved at the language attributed to him was at liberty to claim the protection of the House. When legislators and executive were so sensitive, it was hardly likely that the great ones, the supposed salt of the earth, should be less thin-skinned. Any kind of criticism upon princes of the blood was looked upon as rank blasphemy; the morals of a not blameless or too reputable aristocracy were guaranteed immunity from attack, while the ecclesiastical hierarchy was apparently not strong enough to vindicate its tenets or position without having recourse to the secular arm.

As time passed, the early martyrs to freedom of speech, such men as Prynne, Bastwick and Daniel Defoe, were followed by many victims to similar oppression. One of the first to suffer after Defoe was the nonjuring clergyman Lawrence Howell, who died in Newgate. He was prosecuted about 1720 for writing a pamphlet in which he denounced George I as a usurper. He was tried at the Old Bailey, convicted, and sentenced to pay a fine of £500 to the king, to find sureties for an additional sum, to be imprisoned in Newgate for three years, and during that term to be twice whipped. He was also to be degraded and stripped of his gown by the common executioner. Howell asked indignantly of his judges, "Who will whip a clergyman?" "We pay no deference to your cloth," replied the court, "because you are a disgrace to it, and have no right to wear it." The validity of his ordination was also denied by the court, and as Howell continued to protest, the hangman was ordered to tear off his gown as he stood there at the Bar. The public whipping was not inflicted, but Howell died soon afterwards in Newgate.

Next came Nathaniel Mist, who was sentenced in 1721 to stand in the pillory, to pay a fine, and suffer imprisonment for reflecting upon the action of George I as regards the Protestants in the Palatinate. His paper, the *Weekly Journal* or *Saturday's Post*, was notoriously Jacobite in its views. Soon afterwards he came under the displeasure of the House of Commons for instituting comparisons between the times of the rebellion of 1715 and those which followed, and was committed to Newgate for uttering a "false, malicious, and scandalous libel." This interference by the House with Mist's publications in a matter which did not concern its privileges is characterized by Hallam as an extraordinary assumption of parliamentary power. Tom Paine, whose rationalist writings gained him much obloquy later on, was one of the next in point of time to feel the arm of the law. In 1724 he was convicted of three libels on the Government, fined £100, and imprisoned for a year. A clergyman, William Rowland, was put in the pillory in 1729 for commenting too freely in print on two magistrates who had failed to convict and punish prisoners charged with unnatural crimes. Mr. Rowland was pilloried in his canonical habit, and preached all the time to the multitude, complaining of the injustice of his sentence, whereupon the people, amongst whom were several women, made a collection for him.

About 1730, newspapers were especially established for purposes of political party warfare, and each side libelled or prosecuted the other in turn. The *Craftsman* about this date sprang into the first rank for wit and invective. Its editors were constantly in trouble; the statesmen who supported it had to defend their bantling with their swords. In 1738 the printer, Henry Haines, was sentenced to two years' imprisonment for producing the paper. In 1759 Dr. Shebbeare was fined, put in the pillory, and imprisoned for three years, his offence being the publication of what was deemed a scandalous libel in his "Sixth Letter to the English People." Four years later, John Wilkes, M. P., started the *North Briton*, a Liberal print, in opposition to Smollet's *Briton*, a Tory paper, which was subsidized and supported by Lord Bute, then in power. John Wilkes was no doubt assisted by Lord Temple and John Churchill the satirist. The *North Briton* had been intended to assail Lord Bute's government, but it was not until its forty-fifth number that the dash and boldness of its contributors attracted general attention. In this number a writer rashly accused the king of falsehood. The matter was at once taken up; proceedings were instituted against printer and publisher, who were arrested, as was also Wilkes. These arrests subsequently formed the subject of lengthy lawsuits; they were in the end declared illegal, and all three got heavy damages. Wilkes was, however, expelled from the House, by whose order the offending numbers of the *North Briton* were burnt by the common hangman. But these measures did not extinguish the *North Briton*, which was continued as far as the two hundred and seventeenth number, when Mr. William Bingley, a bookseller, who at that time owned it, was committed to Newgate, and kept there a couple of years for refusing to reply to interrogatories connected with an earlier number of the paper. Wilkes, who had fled to France to escape imprisonment, next fell under the displeasure of the House of Lords. The *London Evening Post*, a paper which had already come into collision with the Commons for presuming to publish reports of debates, committed the seemingly venial offence of inserting a letter from Wilkes, in which he commented rather freely upon a peer of the realm at that time British Ambassador in Paris. The House of Lords could not touch Wilkes, but they took proceedings against the printer for breach of privilege in presuming to mention the name of one of its members, and fined him £100. The precedent soon became popular, and in succeeding sessions printers were constantly fined whenever they mentioned, even by accident, the name of a peer.

Journalism was in these days an ill-used profession. The reign of George III must always be remembered as a time when newspapers and those who wrote them were at the mercy of the people in power. Grant declares that the despotic and tyrannical treatment of the press during the several administrations under George III had no parallel in English history. The executive was capriciously sensitive to criticism, and readily roused to extreme measures. No newspaper indeed was safe; the editors of Liberal prints, or their contributors, who touched on political subjects were at the mercy of the Attorney-General. Any morning's issue might be made the subject of a prosecution, and every independent writer on the wrong side went in daily dread of fine, the pillory, or committal to Newgate. Among the early records of the great organ which custom has long honoured with the title of the "leading journal," are several instances of the dangers journalists encountered. The *Daily Universal Register*, started by the first Mr. John Walter in 1785, became the *Times* in 1788. On the 11th July, 1789, the publisher of the paper—at that time Mr. Walter himself—was tried and convicted of alleged libels on three royal dukes, York, Gloucester, and Cumberland, whose joy at the recovery of the king the *Times* dared to characterize as insincere. The sentence decreed and inflicted was a fine of £50, imprisonment in Newgate for one year, and exposure on the pillory at Charing Cross. A second prosecution followed, intended to protect, and if possible rehabilitate, the Prince of Wales, and Mr. Walter, having been brought from Newgate for the trial, was sentenced to a further fine of £100, and a like sum for a libel on the Duke of Clarence. Mr. Walter remained in Newgate for eighteen months, and was released in March, 1791, having been pardoned at the instance of the Prince of Wales.

Nor was the law invoked in favour of these princes alone. A few years later a foreign monarch obtained equal protection, and the editor, printer, and publisher of the *Courier* were fined and imprisoned for stigmatizing the Czar of Russia as a tyrant among his own subjects, and ridiculous to the rest of Europe. The House of Peers, including the Bench of Bishops, continued very sensitive. In 1799 the printer of the *Cambridge Intelligence* was brought to the bar of the House, charged with reflecting on the speech of the Bishop of Llandaff concerning the union with Ireland. Lord Grenville moved that the printer should be fined £100 and committed to Newgate; Lord Holland protested, but it was justified by Lord Kenyon, and the motion was carried. Lord Kenyon did not spare the unfortunates arraigned before him for libel. One Thomas Spence, who published a pamphlet called "Spence's Restorer of Society," in which the abolition of private ownership of land was advocated, and its investment in parishes for the good of the public at large, was brought before Lord Kenyon, and sentenced by him to twelve months' imprisonment and a fine of £50. Another peer, Lord Ellenborough, who prosecuted Messrs. White and Hart for a libel in 1808, obtained a conviction against them, and a sentence of three years' imprisonment.

In 1810 the House of Commons distinguished itself by a prosecution which led to rather serious consequences. At a debate on the Walcheren expedition, a member, Mr. Yorke, had insisted from day to day upon the exclusion of strangers, and another, Mr. Windham, had inveighed violently against press reporting. Upon this a question was discussed at a debating society known as the "British Forum," as to whether Mr. Yorke's or Mr. Windham's conduct was the greater outrage on the public feeling. The decision was given against Mr. Yorke, and the result announced in a placard outside. This placard was constituted a breach of privilege, comment upon the proceedings of the House being deemed a contravention of the Bill of Rights. A Mr. John Gale Jones confessing himself the author of the placard, he was forthwith committed to Newgate. Sir Francis Burdett took Jones's part, and published his protest, signed, in Cobbett's *Weekly Register*. The House on this ordered the Sergeant-at-arms to arrest Sir Francis and take him to the Tower. Sir Francis resisted, and was carried off by force. A riot occurred *en route*, the crowd attacked the escort, and the troops fired, with fatal consequences, upon the crowd. Sir Francis appealed to the law courts, which in the end refused to take cognizance of the questions at issue, and he was released, returning home in triumph. Mr. John Gale Jones claimed to be tried, and refused to leave Newgate without it; but he was got out by a stratagem, loudly complaining that he had been illegally imprisoned, and illegally thrust out. Jones was sentenced in the autumn of the same year to twelve months' imprisonment in Coldbath Fields Gaol. Another and a better known writer found himself in Newgate about this time. In 1810 William Cobbett was tried for animadverting too openly upon the indignity of subjecting English soldiers to corporal punishment, for which he was sentenced to two years' imprisonment in Newgate, and a fine of £1000. This was not his first prosecution, but it was by far the most serious. Shorter sentences of imprisonment were imposed on his printers and publishers, Messrs. Hansard, Budd, and Bagshaw.

Some other notable criminals found themselves in Newgate about this date. In 1809 it became the place of punishment for two Government officials who were convicted of embezzlement on a large scale. The first, Mr. Alexander Davison, was employed to purchase barrack-stores for the Government on commission. He was intrusted with this duty by the barrack-master general, as a person of extensive mercantile experience, to avoid the uncertainty of trusting to contractors. Mr. Davison was to receive a commission of two and one-half per cent. Instead of buying in the best and cheapest markets, he became also the seller, thus making a profit on the goods and receiving the commission as well; or, in the words of Mr. Justice

Grose, Davison, when "receiving a stipend to check the frauds of others, and insure the best commodities at the cheapest rate, became the tradesman and seller of the article, and had thereby an interest to increase his own profit, and to commit that fraud it was his duty to prevent." Davison disgorged some £18,000 of his ill-won profits, and this was taken into consideration in his sentence, which was limited to imprisonment in Newgate for twenty-one months. The other delinquent was Mr. Valentine Jones, who had been appointed commissary-general and superintendent of forage and provisions in the West Indies in 1795. A large British force was at that time stationed in the West Indian Islands, which entailed vast disbursements from the public exchequer. The whole of this money passed through the hands of Mr. Jones. His career of fraud began as soon as he took over his duties. Mr. Higgins, a local merchant, came to him proposing to renew contracts for the supply of the troops, but Mr. Jones would only consent to their renewal on condition that he shared Mr. Higgins' profits. Higgins protested, but at length yielded. Within three years the enormous sum of £87,000 sterling was paid over to Jones as his share in this nefarious transaction. Mr. Jones was tried at the King's Bench and sentenced to three years' imprisonment in Newgate.

Soon afterwards a person of very high rank was committed to Newgate. This was the Marquis of Sligo, who was convicted of enticing British men-of-war's-men to desert, and sentenced to imprisonment, with a fine of £5000. Lord Sligo went to Malta soon after leaving college, and there hired a brig, the *Pylades*, intending to make a yachting tour in the Grecian Archipelago. The admiral at Malta and other naval officers helped Lord Sligo to fit out the *Pylades*, and he was welcomed on board the various king's ships. From one of these several trusty seamen were shortly afterwards missing. Their captain trusted to Lord Sligo's honour that he had not decoyed these men, and that he would not receive them; but at that moment the deserters were actually on board the *Pylades*, having been enticed from the service by Lord Sligo's servants. The *Pylades* then went on her cruise along the Mediterranean. Suspicion seems still to have rested on Lord Sligo, and after leaving Palermo the *Pylades* was chased and brought to by H. M. S. *Active*. A boat boarded the *Pylades*, her crew was mustered and examined, but the deserters had been securely hidden in the after hold, and were not discovered. A little later Lord Sligo sailed for Patmos, where some of the crew landed and were left behind; among them were the men-of-war's-men, through whom the whole affair was brought to light. Lord Sligo was arrested on his return to England, and tried at the Old Bailey. The evidence was conclusive. In the course of the trial a letter was put in from Lord Sligo, to the effect that if the business was brought into court he should do his best to defend himself; if he did not succeed, he had an ample fortune, and could pay the fines. No money, however, could save him from incarceration, and in accordance with the sentence of Sir William Scott, who was supported on the bench by Lord

Ellenborough and Mr. Baron Thompson, the Marquis of Sligo was sent to Newgate for four months.

FOOTNOTES:

[82:1] The sobriquet of Gentleman Harry was also enjoyed by Henry Simms, a highwayman who frequented the Lewisham and Blackheath roads. On one occasion, when travelling into Northamptonshire on a rather fresh horse, a gentleman who was in a post-chaise remarked to him, "Don't ride so hard, sir, or you'll soon ride away all your estate." "Indeed I shall not," replied Simms, "for it lies in several counties," and dismounting, he challenged the gentleman to stand, and robbed him of a hundred and two guineas.

CHAPTER IV
NEWGATE IN THE NINETEENTH CENTURY

Newgate still overcrowded—Description of interior—Debtors in Middlesex—Debtors in Newgate—Fees extorted—Garnish—Scanty food—Little bedding—Squalor and wretchedness prevail throughout—Constant quarrels and fighting—Discipline maintained only by prisoner wardsmen—Their tyranny and extortion—A new debtors' prison indispensable—Building of Whitecross Street—The criminal side—Indiscriminate association of all classes—The press-yard—Recklessness of the condemned—Cashman—The condemned cells—Summary of glaring defects in Newgate—Crimes constantly being hatched in Newgate—The Corporation roused to reform Newgate—Little accomplished.

With criminals and misdemeanants of all shades crowding perpetually into its narrow limits, the latter state of Newgate was worse than the first. The new gaol fell as far short of the demands made on it as did the old. The prison population fluctuated a great deal, but it was almost always in excess of the accommodation available, and there were times when the place was full to overflowing. At one time there were three hundred debtors and nine hundred criminals in Newgate, or twelve hundred prisoners in all.

In order to realize the evils entailed by incarceration in Newgate in these days, it is necessary to give some account of its interior as it was occupied and appropriated in 1810. The gaol at that date was divided into eight separate and more or less distinct departments, each of which had its own wards and yard. These were as follows: the male debtors' side; the female debtors' side; the chapel yard; the middle yard; the master felons' side; the female felons' side; the state side; and the press-yard.

The squalor and uncleanness of the debtors' side was intensified by constant overcrowding. Prisoners were committed to it quite without reference to its capacity. No remonstrance was attended to, no steps taken to reduce the number of committals, and the governor was obliged to utilize the chapel as a day and night room for them. Besides this, although the families of debtors were no longer permitted to live with them inside the gaol, hundreds of women and children came in every morning to spend the day in the prison, and there was no limitation to the numbers of visitors admitted to the debtors' side. Friends arrived about nine in the morning, and went out at nine o'clock at night, when as many as two hundred visitors have been observed leaving the debtors' yards at one time. The day passed in revelry and drunkenness. Although spirituous liquors were forbidden, wine and beer might be had in any quantity, the only limitation being that not more than one bottle of wine or one quart of beer could be issued at one time. No account was taken of the amount of liquors admitted in one day, and debtors might practically have as much as they liked, if they could only pay for it. No attempt was made to check drunkenness, beyond the penalty of shutting out friends from any ward in which a prisoner exceeded. Quarrelling among the debtors was not unfrequent. Blows were struck, and fights often ensued. For this and other acts of misconduct there was the discipline of the refractory ward, or "strong room" on the debtors' side. Bad cases were removed to a cell on the felons' side, and here they were locked in solitary confinement for three days at a time.

Order throughout the debtors' side was preserved and discipline maintained by a system open to grave abuses, which had the prescription of long usage, and which was never wholly rooted out for many years to come. This was the pernicious plan of governing by prisoners, or of setting a favoured few in authority over the many. The head of the debtors' prison was a prisoner called the steward, who was chosen by the whole body from six whom the keeper nominated. This steward was practically supreme. All the allowances of food passed through his hands; he had the control of the poor-box for chance charities, he collected the garnish money, and distributed the weekly grant from the prison charitable fund.

The criminal side of Newgate consisted of the six quarters or yards, and the inmates, distinguished from the debtors, were comprised in four classes: those awaiting trial; persons under sentence of imprisonment for a fixed period, or until they shall have paid certain fines; transports awaiting removal to the colonies, and capital convicts, condemned to death and awaiting execution. At one time all of these different categories were thrown together pell-mell, young and old, the untried with the convicted. An imperfect attempt at classification was, however, made in 1812, and a yard was as far as possible set apart for the untried, or the class, with whom, under the imperious demand for accommodation, were also associated the misdemeanants. This was the chapel yard, with its five wards, which were calculated to accommodate seventy prisoners, but often held many more. A further sub-classification was attempted by separating at night those charged with misdemeanours from those charged with felony, but all mingled freely during the day in the yard. The sleeping accommodation in the chapel-yard wards, and indeed throughout the prison, consisted of a barrack bed, which was a wooden flooring on a slightly inclined plane, with a beam running across the top to serve as a pillow. No beds were allowed, only two rugs per prisoner. When each sleeper had the full lateral space allotted to him, it amounted to one foot and a half on the barrack bed; but when the ward was obliged to accommodate double the ordinary number, as was frequently the case, the sleepers covered the entire floor, with the exception of a passage in the middle. All the misdemeanants, whatever their offence, were lodged in this chapel ward. As many various and, according to our ideas, heinous crimes came under this head, in the then existing state of the law, the man guilty of a common assault found himself side by side with the fraudulent, or others who had attempted abominable crimes. In this heterogeneous society were also thrown the unfortunate journalists to whom reference has already been made.

The middle yard, as far as its limits would permit, was appropriated to felons and transports. The wards here were generally very crowded. Constantly associated with these convicted felons were numbers of juveniles, infants of tender years. There were frequently in the middle yard seven or eight children, the youngest barely nine, the oldest only twelve or thirteen, exposed to all the contaminating influences of the place. Mr. Bennet mentions also the case of young men of better stamp, clerks in city offices, and youths of good parentage, "in this dreadful situation," who had been rescued from the hulks through the kindness and attention of the Secretary of State. "Yet they had been long enough," he goes on to say, "in the prison associated with the lowest and vilest criminals, with convicts of all ages and characters, to render it next to impossible but that, with the obliteration of all sense of self-respect, the inevitable consequence of such a situation, their morals must have been destroyed; . . . the lessons they were taught in this academy, must have had a tendency to turn them into the world hardened and accomplished in the ways of vice and crime."

Felons who could pay the price were permitted, irrespective of their character or offences, to purchase the greater ease and comfort of the master's side. The entrance fee was at least 13s. 6d. a head, with half-a-crown a week more for bed and bedding, the wards being furnished with barrack bedsteads, upon which each prisoner had the regulation allowance of sleeping room, or about a foot and a half laterally. These fees were in reality a substantial contribution towards the expenses of the gaol; without them the keeper declared that he could not pay the salaries of turnkeys and servants, nor keep the prison going at all. Besides the gaol fees, there was "garnish" of half-a-guinea, collected by the steward, and spent in providing coals, candles, plates, knives, and forks; while all the occupants of this part of the prison supported themselves; they had the ration of prison bread only, but they had no share in the prison meat or other charities, and they or their friends found them in food. All who could scrape together the cash seem to have gladly availed themselves of the privilege of entering the master's side. It was the only way to escape the horrors, the distress, penury, and rags of the common yards. Idleness was not so universally the rule in this part of the gaol. Artisans and others were at liberty to work at their trades, provided they were not dangerous. Tailoring and shoemaking were permitted, but it was deemed unsafe to allow a carpenter or blacksmith to have his tools. All the money earned by prisoners was at their own disposal, and was spent almost habitually in drink and wantonness.

The best accommodation the gaol could offer was reserved for the prisoners on the state side, from whom still higher fees were exacted, with the same discreditable idea of swelling the revenues of the prison. To constitute this the aristocratic quarter, unwarrantable demands were made upon the space properly allotted to the female felons, and no lodger was rejected, whatever his status, who offered himself and could bring grist to the mill. The luxury of the state side was for a long time open to all who could pay—the convicted felon, the transport awaiting removal, the lunatic whose case was still undecided, the misdemeanant tried or untried, the debtor who wished to avoid the discomfort of the crowded debtors' side, the outspoken newspaper editor, or the daring reporter of parliamentary debates. The better class of inmate complained bitterly of this enforced companionship with the vile, association at one time forbidden by custom, but which greed and rapacity long made the rule. The fee for admission to the state side, as fixed by the table of fees, was three guineas, but Mr. Newman declared that he never took more than two. Ten and sixpence a week more was charged as rent for a single bed; where two or more slept in a bed the rent was seven shillings a week each. Prisoners who could afford it sometimes paid for four beds, at the rate of twenty-eight shillings, and so secured the luxury of a private room. A Mr. Lundy, charged with forgery, was thus accommodated on the state side for upwards of five years. But the keeper protested that no single prisoner could thus monopolize space if the state side was crowded. The keeper went still further in his efforts to make money. He continued the ancient practice of letting out a portion of his own house, and by a poetical fiction treated it as an annex of the state side. Mr. Davison, sent to Newgate for embezzlement, was accommodated with a room in Mr. Newman's house at the extravagant rental of thirty guineas per week; Mr. Cobbett was also a lodger of Mr. Newman's; and so were any members of the aristocracy, if they happened to be in funds.

The female felons' wards were always full to overflowing; sometimes double the number the rooms could accommodate were crowded into them. There was a master's side for females who could pay the usual fees, but they associated with the rest in the one narrow yard common to all. The tried and the untried, young and old, were herded together; sometimes girls of thirteen, twelve, even ten or nine years of age, were exposed to all the contagion and profligacy which prevailed in this part of the prison. There was no separation even for the women under sentence of death, who lived in a common and perpetually crowded ward. Only when the order of execution came down were those about to suffer placed apart in one of the rooms in the arcade of the middle ward.

The press-yard was the receptacle of the male condemned prisoners and was generally crowded, like the rest of the prison. Except in murder cases, where the execution was generally very promptly performed, strange and inconceivable delay occurred in carrying out the extreme sentences. Hence there was a terrible accumulation of prisoners in the condemned cells. Once, during the long illness of George III, as many as one hundred were there waiting the "Report," as it was called. At another time there were fifty, one of whom had been under sentence a couple of years. Mr. Bennet speaks of thirty-eight capital convicts he found in the press-yard in February, 1817, five of whom had been condemned the previous July, four in September, and twenty-nine in October. This procrastination bred a certain callousness. Few realizing that the dreadful fate would overtake them, dismissed the prospect of death, and until the day was actually fixed, spent the time in roystering, swearing, gambling, or playing at ball. Visitors were permitted access to them without stint; unlimited drink was not denied them provided it was obtained in regulated quantities at one time. These capital convicts, says Mr. Bennet, "lessened the ennui and despair of their situation by unbecoming merriment, or sought relief in the constant application of intoxicating stimulants. I saw Cashman[125:1] a few hours before his execution, smoking and drinking with the utmost unconcern and indifference." Those who were thus reckless reacted upon the penitent who knew their days were numbered, and their gibes and jollity counteracted the ordinary's counsels or the independent preacher's earnest prayers. For while Roman Catholics and Dissenters were encouraged to see ministers of their own persuasion, a number of amateurs were ever ready to give their gratuitous ministrations to the condemned.

The prisoners in the press-yard had free access during the day to the yard and large day room; at night they were placed in the fifteen cells, two, three, or more together, according to the total number to be accommodated. They were never left quite alone for fear of suicide, and for the same reason they were searched for weapons or poisons. But they nevertheless frequently managed to secrete the means of making away with themselves, and thus accomplished their purpose. Convicted murderers were kept continuously in the cells on bread and water, in couples, from the time of sentence to that of execution, which was about three or four days generally, from Friday to Monday, so as to include one Sunday, on which day there was a special service for the condemned in the prison chapel. This latter was an ordeal which all dreaded, and many avoided by denying their faith. The condemned occupied an open pew in the centre of the chapel, hung with black; in front of them, upon a table, was a black coffin in full view. The chapel was filled with a curious but callous congregation, who came to stare at the miserable people thus publicly exposed. Well might Mr. Bennet write that the condition of the condemned side was the most prominent of the manifold evils in the present system of Newgate, so discreditable to the metropolis.

The report of the Committee of the House of Commons painted so black a picture of Newgate as then conducted, that the Corporation were roused in very shame to undertake some kind of reform. The above-mentioned report was ordered to be printed upon the 9th of May. Upon the 29th of July the same year, the court of aldermen appointed a committee of its own body, assisted by the town clerk, Mr. Dance, city surveyor, son of the architect of Newgate, and Mr. Addison, keeper of Newgate, to make a visitation of the gaols supposed to be the best managed, including those of Petworth and Gloucester.[127:1]

After much anxious consideration certain improvements were introduced. The state side ceased to exist, and the female prisoners thus regained the space of which their quadrangle had been robbed. The privileges of the master's side also disappeared; fees were nominally abolished, and garnish was scotched, although not yet killed outright. A certain number of bedsteads were provided, and there was a slight increase in the ration of bread. But now the Corporation took alarm at the terrible expense adequate reform would entail and hence the most crying evils were left untouched. If a metropolitan prison were to be erected on the same lines as the recently built prisons of Gloucester and Petworth, with all the space not only for air and exercise, but for day rooms and sleeping cells, it would cover some thirty acres, and cost a great deal more than the city could possibly afford; therefore nothing was done.

FOOTNOTES:

[125:1] Cashman was the only one of the Spafields rioters (1816) who was capitally convicted and executed. Four others who were arraigned with him were acquitted by the jury, to the astonishment of the court. Cashman, who had been a seaman in the Royal Navy, pleaded that he had been to the Admiralty to claim prize-money to the value of £200 on the day of the riot. On his way home, half drunk, he had been persuaded to join the rioters. Cashman's unconcern lasted to the end. As he appeared on the gallows the mob groaned and hissed the Government, and Cashman joined in the outcry until the drop fell.

[127:1] Petworth Prison, built in 1785, and Gloucester Penitentiary, erected in 1791, were the two first gaols established which provided a separate sleeping cell for every prisoner.

CHAPTER V
PHILANTHROPIC EFFORTS

Absence of religious and moral instruction in Newgate a hundred years ago—Chaplains not always zealous—Amateur enthusiasts minister to the prisoners—Silas Told, his life and work—Wesley leads him to prison visitation—Goes to Newgate regularly—Attends the condemned to the gallows—Alexander Cruden of the "Concordance" also visits Newgate—A neglectful Chaplain—Private philanthropy active—Various societies formed—Prison schools—The female side the most disgraceful part of the prison—Elizabeth Fry's first visit—The School—The Matron—Work obtained—Rules framed—Female prison reformed—Newgate on exhibition.

Among the many drawbacks from which the inmates of Newgate suffered through the eighteenth and the early part of the nineteenth centuries, was the absence of proper religious and moral instruction. The value of the ministrations of the ordinary, who was the official ghostly adviser, entirely depended upon his personal qualities. Now and again he was an earnest and devoted man, to whom the prisoners might fully open their hearts. More often he was careless and indifferent, satisfied to earn his salary by the slightest and most perfunctory discharge of his sacred duties. There were ordinaries whose fame rested rather upon their powers of digestion than polemics or pulpit oratory. The Newgate chaplain had to say grace at city banquets, and was sometimes called upon to eat three consecutive dinners without rising from the table. One in particular was noted for his skill in compounding a salad, another for his jovial companionship. But the ordinary took life easy, and beyond conducting the services, did little work. Only when executions were imminent was he especially busy. It behooved him then to collect matter for his account of the previous life and misdeeds of the condemned, and their demeanour at Tyburn; and this, according to contemporary records, led him to get all the information he could from the malefactors who passed through his hands.

But while the official chaplain lacked zeal or religious fervour, there were not wanting others more earnest and enthusiastic to add their unprofessional but devoted efforts to the half-hearted ministrations of the ordinary of Newgate. A prominent figure in the philanthropic annals of Newgate is that of Silas Told, who devoted many years of his life to the spiritual needs of the prisoners. Told's career is full of peculiar interest. He was a pious child; both father and mother were religious folk, and brought him up carefully. According to his own memoirs, when quite an infant he and his sister

Dulcibella were wont to wander into the woods and fields to converse about "God and happiness." Told passed through many trials and vicissitudes in his early years. At thirteen he went to sea as an apprentice, and suffered much ill-usage. He made many voyages to the West Indies and to the Guinea coast, being a horrified and unwilling witness of some of the worst phases of the slave trade. He fell into the hands of piratical Spaniards, was cast away on a reef, saved almost by a miracle, last of all was pressed on board a man-of-war. Here, on board H. M. S. *Phœnix* his religious tendencies were strengthened by a pious captain, and presently he married and left the sea for ever. After this he became a schoolmaster in Essex, then a clerk and book-keeper in London. Here he came under the influence of John Wesley, and although predisposed against the Methodists, he was profoundly impressed by their leader's preaching. While listening to a sermon by John Wesley on the suddenness of conversion, Told heard another voice say to him, "This is the truth," and from that time forth he became a zealous Methodist.

It was Wesley who led him to prison visitation. He was at that time schoolmaster of the Foundry school, and his call to his long and devoted labours in Newgate were brought about in this wise. "In the year 1744," to quote his own words, "I attended the children one morning at the five o'clock preaching, when Mr. Wesley took his text out of the twenty-fifth chapter of St. Matthew. When he read 'I was sick and in prison, and ye visited me not,' I was sensible of my negligence in never visiting the prisoners during the course of my life, and was filled with horror of mind beyond expression. This threw me well-nigh into a state of despondency, as I was totally unacquainted with the measures requisite to be pursued for that purpose. However, the gracious God, two or three days after, sent a messenger to me in the school, who informed me of the malefactors that were under sentence of death, and would be glad of any of our friends who could go and pray with them. . . . In consequence, I committed my school to my trusty usher, and went to Newgate."

After this first visit he went there regularly. He described the place twenty-one years later, but still remembered it vividly, as "such an emblem of the infernal pit as he never saw before." However, he struggled bravely on, having a constant pressure upon his mind "to stand up for God in the midst of them," and praying much for wisdom and fortitude. He preached as often as he was permitted to both felons and debtors. But for the first few years, when attending the malefactors, he met with so many repulses from the keeper and ordinary, as well as from the prisoners themselves, that he was often greatly discouraged. "But notwithstanding I more vehemently pressed through all, becoming the more resolute and taking no denial."

He continued his labours for many years, and in 1767 he visited the notorious Mrs. Brownrigg, who was sentenced to be hanged for whipping her servant-maid to death, and whom he accompanied to the gallows. His death occurred in 1779. He lived to hear of Howard's philanthropic exertions, and to see the introduction of some small measure of prison reform.

While Silas Told was thus engaged, another but a more erratic and eccentric philanthropist paid constant visits to Newgate. This was Alexander Cruden, the well-known, painstaking compiler of the "Concordance." For a long time he came daily to the gaol, to preach and instruct the prisoners in the gospel, rewarding the most diligent and attentive with money, till he found that the cash thus disbursed was often spent in drink the moment his back was turned. Through Mr. Cruden's solicitations a sentence of death upon a forger, Richard Potter, was commuted to one of transportation.

More precise details of the manner in which a Newgate ordinary interpreted his trust will be found in the evidence of the Rev. Brownlow Forde, LL. D., before the committee of 1814. Dr. Forde took life pretty easy. Had a prisoner sent for him, he told the committee, he might have gone, but as they did not send, unless they were sick and thought themselves at death's door, he confined his ministrations to the condemned, whom he visited twice a week in the day room of the press-yard, or daily after the order for execution had arrived. He repudiated the notion that he had anything to do with the state of morals of the gaol. He felt no obligation to instruct youthful prisoners, or attend to the spiritual needs of the little children so often thrown into Newgate. He never went to the infirmary unless sent for, and did not consider it his duty to visit the sick, and often knew nothing of a prisoner's illness unless he was warned to attend the funeral. Among other reasons, he said that as the turnkeys were always busy, there was no one to attend him. While the chaplain was thus careless and apathetic, the services he conducted were little likely to be edifying or decorous. The most disgraceful scenes were common in the prison chapel. As the prisoners trooped into the galleries they shouted and halloed to their friends in the body of the church. Friends interchanged greetings, and "How d'ye do, Sall?" was answered by "Gallows well, Conkey Beau," as the men recognized their female acquaintances, and were recognized in turn. The congregation might be pretty quiet after the chaplain had made his appearance, but more often it was disorderly from first to last. Any disposed to behave well were teased and laughed at by others. Unrestricted conversation went on, accompanied by such loud yawning, laughing, or coughing as almost impeded the service. No one in authority attempted to preserve order; the gatesmen, themselves prisoners, might expostulate, but the turnkeys who were present ignored any disturbance until reminded of their duty by the chaplain. The keeper never attended service. It was suggested to him that he might have a pew in the chapel with a private entrance to it from his own house, but nothing came of the proposal. It was not incumbent upon the prisoners, except those condemned to death, to attend chapel. Sometimes it was crowded, sometimes there was hardly a soul. In severe weather the place, in which there was no fire, was nearly empty. It was very lofty, very cold, and the prisoners, ill clad, did not care to shiver through the service. On "curiosity days," those of the condemned sermon, more came, including debtors and visitors from outside, who thronged to see the demeanour of the wretched convicts under the painful circumstances already described. The service must have been conducted in a very slovenly and irreverent manner. Dr. Forde had no clerk, unless it chanced that some one in the condemned pew knew how to read. If not, there were sometimes no responses, and the whole service was apt to be thrown into confusion.

Dr. Forde seems to have been more in his element when taking the chair at a public-house "free-and-easy." In the "Book for a Rainy Day," Mr. Smith gives us an account of a visit which was paid to Dr. Forde at a public-house in Hatton Garden. "Upon entering the club-room, we found the Doctor most pompously seated in a superb masonic chair, under a stately crimson canopy placed between the windows. The room was clouded with smoke, whiffed to the ceiling, which gave me a better idea of what I had heard of the 'Black Hole of Calcutta' than any place I had seen. There were present at least a hundred associates of every denomination."

It is consoling to find that while officials slumbered, private philanthropy was active, and had been in some cases for years. Various societies and institutions had been set on foot to assist and often replace public justice in dealing with criminals. The Marine Society grew out of a subscription started by Justices Fielding and Welch, in 1756, for the purpose of clothing vagrant and friendless lads and sending them on board the fleet. The Philanthropic Society had been established in 1789 by certain benevolent persons to supply a home for destitute boys and girls, and this admirable institution steadily grew and prospered. In 1794 it moved to larger premises, and in 1817 it had an income of £6000 a year, partly from subscriptions and legacies, partly from the profit on labour executed by its inmates.[135.1] In 1816 another body of well-meaning people, moved by the alarming increase of juvenile delinquency in the metropolis, formed a society to investigate its causes, inquire into the individual cases of boys actually under sentence, and afford such relief upon release as might appear deserved or likely to prevent a relapse into crime. The members of this society drew up a list containing seven hundred names of the friends and associates of boys in Newgate, all of whom they visited and sought to reform. They went further, and seriously discussed the propriety of establishing a special penitentiary for juveniles, a scheme which was not completely carried out. Another institution was the Refuge for the Destitute, which took in boys and girls on their discharge from prison, to teach them trades and give them a fair start in life. There were also the Magdalen Hospital and the Female Penitentiary, both of which did good work amongst depraved women.

Matters had improved somewhat in Newgate after the report of the committee in 1814, at least as regards the juveniles. A school had been established, over which the new ordinary, Mr. Cotton, who about this time succeeded Dr. Forde, presided, and in which he took a great interest. The chaplain was in communication with the Philanthropic and other institutions, and promising cases were removed to them. The boys were kept as far as possible apart from the men, but not at first from one another. Hence in the one long room they occupied and used for all purposes, eating, drinking, and sleeping, the elder and more vitiated boys were still able to exercise a baneful influence over the young and innocent. More space became available by the removal of the debtors to Whitecross Street, and then the boys were lodged according to classes in four different rooms. Mr. Cotton believed that the boys benefitted morally from the instruction and care they received. This juvenile school was the one bright spot in the prevailing darkness of Newgate at that particular time. Another and a still more remarkable amelioration in the condition of the prisoners was soon to attract universal attention. The great and good work accomplished by that noble woman Mrs. Fry on the female side of Newgate forms an epoch in prison history, and merits a particular description.

Bad as were the other various courts and so called "sides" in Newgate prison, the quadrangle appropriated to the females was far worse. Its foul and degraded condition had attracted the sympathies of Elizabeth Fry as early as 1813. The winter had been unusually severe, and Mrs. Fry had been induced by several Friends, particularly by William Forster, to visit Newgate and endeavour to alleviate the sufferings of the female prisoners. The space allotted to the women was at that time still curtailed by the portion given over to the state side. They were limited to two wards and two cells, an area of about one hundred and ninety-two superficial yards in all, into which, at the time of Mrs. Fry's visit, some three hundred women with their children were crowded, all classes together, felon and misdemeanant, tried and untried; the whole under the superintendence of an old man and his son. They slept on the floor, without so much as a mat for bedding. Many were very nearly naked, others were in rags; some desperate from want of food, some savage from drink, foul in language, still more recklessly depraved in their habits and behaviour. Everything was filthy beyond description. The smell of the place was quite disgusting. The keeper himself, Mr. Newman, was reluctant to go amongst them. He strove hard to dissuade Mrs. Fry from entering the wards, and failing in that, begged her at least to leave her watch in his office, assuring her that not even his presence would prevent its being torn from her. Mrs. Fry's own account fully endorses all this. "All I tell thee is a faint picture of the reality; the filth, the closeness of the rooms, the ferocious manners and expressions of the women towards each other, and the abandoned wickedness which everything bespoke, are quite indescribable." "One act, the account of which I received from another quarter, marks the degree of wretchedness to which they were reduced at that time. Two women were seen in the act of stripping a dead child for the purpose of clothing a living one."

Mrs. Fry made other visits, for she wrote under date Feb. 16th, 1813: "Yesterday we were some hours in Newgate with the poor female felons, attending to their outward necessities; we had been twice previously. Before we went away dear Anna Buxton uttered a few words in supplication, and very unexpectedly to myself I did also. I heard weeping, and I thought they appeared much tendered. A very solemn quiet was observed; it was a striking scene, with the poor people around in their deplorable condition." Mrs. Fry's charity extended to the gift of clothing, for it is recorded in her memoirs that many members of her domestic circle had long a vivid recollection of the "green baize garments," and their pleasure in assisting to prepare them.

Nearly four years elapsed before Elizabeth Fry resumed her visits. Newgate and what she had seen there had no doubt made a deep impression on her mind, but a long illness and family afflictions had prevented her from giving her philanthropic yearnings full play. She appears to have recommenced her visits about Christmas, 1816, and on Feb. 16th, 1817, there is an entry in her journal to the effect that she had been "lately much occupied in forming a school in Newgate for the children of the poor prisoners, as well as the young criminals." It was in this way that she struck at the hearts of these poor degraded wretches, who were only too eager to save their children from a life of crime. "The proposal was received even by the most abandoned with tears of joy," says Mrs. Fry. The three intervening years between 1813 and 1816 had brought no improvement in the female side. Its inmates—the very scum of the town—were filthy in their habits and disgusting in their persons. Mrs. Fry tells us she found the railings in the inner yard crowded with half-naked women, struggling together for the front situations with the most boisterous violence, and begging with the utmost vociferation. As double gratings had now been fixed at some distance apart to prevent close communication between prisoners and their visitors, the women had fastened wooden spoons to the end of long sticks, which they thrust across the space as they clamoured for alms. Mrs. Fry says that she felt as if she were going into a den of wild beasts, and that she well recollects quite shuddering when the door closed upon her, and she was locked in with such a herd of novel and desperate companions. The women, according to another eyewitness, sat about the yard on the stones, squalid in attire, ferocious in aspect. On this occasion a woman rushed out from the ward yelling like a wild beast; she made the circuit of the yard, brandishing her arms and tearing the caps or coverings from the heads of the other women. In spite of these terrible scenes, the ladies—several Friends having joined with Mrs. Fry—continued to give their attention to the school. "It was in our visits to the school," she afterwards observed, when giving evidence before the Parliamentary committee of 1818, "where some of us attended every day, that we were witnesses of the dreadful proceedings that went forward on the female side of the prison; the begging, swearing, gaming, fighting, singing, dancing, dressing up in men's clothes; the scenes are too bad to be described, so that we did not think it suitable to admit young persons with us."

It is not strange that these miserable women should be absolutely unsexed. They were often subjected to brutal ill-treatment even before their arrival at Newgate. Many were brought to the prison almost without clothes. If coming from a distance, as in the case of transports lodged in Newgate until embarkation, they were almost invariably ironed, and often cruelly so. One lady saw the female prisoners from Lancaster Castle arrive, not merely handcuffed, but with heavy irons on their legs, which had caused swelling and inflammation. Others wore iron-hoops round their legs and arms, and were chained to each other. On the journey these poor souls could not get up or down from the coach without the whole of them being dragged together. A woman travelled from Cardigan with an iron hoop round her ankle, and fainted when it was removed. This woman's story was, that during a long imprisonment she had worn an iron hoop round her waist, a second round her leg above the knee, a third at the ankle, and all these connected by chains. In the waist hoop were two bolts or fastenings, in which her hands were confined at night when she went to bed. Her bed was only of straw. These wretched and ill-used creatures might be forgiven if they at times broke out into rebellion. For a long time it was the practice with the female transports to riot previous to their departure from Newgate, breaking windows, furniture, or whatever came in their reach. Their outrageous conduct continued all the way from the gaol to the water-side, whither they were conveyed in open wagons, noisy and disorderly to the last, amidst the jeers and shouts of the assembled crowds.

Mrs. Fry, as I have said, endeavoured first to form a school. For this purpose an unoccupied room was set apart by the authorities. Although looking upon her experiment as hopeless, she received cordial support from the sheriffs, the governor, Mr. Newman, and the ordinary of Newgate, Mr. Cotton. The prisoners selected from among themselves a schoolmistress, Mary Connor by name, who had been committed for stealing a watch, and "who proved eminently qualified for her task." The school, which was for children only and young persons under twenty-five, prospered, and by degrees the heroic band of ladies were encouraged to greater efforts. The conduct of the prisoners, their entreaties not to be excluded from the benefits of the school, inspired Mrs. Fry with confidence, and she resolved to attempt the introduction of order, industry, and religious feeling into Newgate. In April, 1817, eleven members of the Society of Friends and another lady, the wife of a clergyman, formed themselves into an association for the improvement of the female prisoners in Newgate.[143:1] These devoted persons gave themselves up entirely to their self-imposed task. With no interval of relaxation, and with but few intermissions from the call of other and more imperious duties, they lived among the prisoners. They arrived, in fact, at the hour of unlocking, and spent the whole day in the prison.

The more crying needs of the Newgate female prison at that date are indicated in a memorandum found among Mrs. Fry's papers. It was greatly in need of room, she said. The women should be under the control and supervision of female, and not, as heretofore, of male officers. The number of visitors should be greatly curtailed, and all communications between prisoners and their friends should take place at stated times, under special rules. The prisoners should not be dependent on their friends for food or clothing, but should have a sufficiency of both from the authorities. Employment should be a part of their punishment, and be provided for them by Government. They might work together in company, but should be separated at night according to classes, under a monitor. Religious instruction should be more closely considered. It was to supply these needs that the committee devoted its efforts, the ladies boldly promising that if a matron could be found who would engage never to leave the prison day or night, they would find employment for the prisoners and the necessary funds until the city could be induced to meet the expense.

The matron was found, and the first prison matron appointed, an elderly respectable woman, who proved competent, and discharged her duties with fidelity. Mrs. Fry next sought the countenance and support of the governor and chaplain, both of whom met her at her husband's house to listen to her views and proposals. Mr. Cotton, the ordinary, was not encouraging; he frankly told her that this, like many other useful and benevolent designs for the improvement of Newgate, would inevitably fail. Mr. Newman, however, bade her not despair; but he afterward confessed that when he came to reflect on the subject, and especially upon the character of the prisoners, he could not see even the possibility of success. Both, however, promised their warmest coöperation. Mrs. Fry next saw one of the sheriffs, asking him to obtain a salary for the matron, and a room in the prison for the Ladies' Committee. This sheriff, Mr. Bridges, was willing to help her if his colleagues and the Corporation agreed, but told her that his concurrence or that of the city would avail her but little—the concurrence of the women themselves was indispensable; and that it was in vain to expect such untamed and turbulent spirits would submit to the regulations of a woman armed with no legal authority, and unable to inflict any punishment. Nevertheless, the two sheriffs met Mrs. Fry at Newgate one Sunday afternoon. The women, seventy in number, were assembled, and asked whether they were prepared to submit to the new rules. All fully and unanimously agreed to abide by them, to the surprise of the sheriffs, who doubted their submitting to such restraints. Upon this the sheriffs addressed the prisoners, telling them that the scheme had official support; then turning to Mrs. Fry, one of the two magistrates said, "Well, ladies, you see your materials."

The evidence of a gentleman who visited Newgate within a fortnight of the adoption of the new rules may fitly be added here. He went one day to call on Mrs. Fry at the prison, and was conducted to the women's side. "On my approach," he says, "no loud or dissonant sounds or angry voices indicated that I was about to enter a place which I was credibly assured had long had for one of its titles that of 'Hell above ground.' The court-yard into which I was admitted, instead of being peopled with beings scarcely human, blaspheming, fighting, tearing each other's hair, or gaming with a filthy pack of cards for the very clothes they wore, which often did not suffice even for decency, presented a scene where stillness and propriety reigned. I was conducted by a decently-dressed person, the newly-appointed yards-woman, to the door of a ward where at the head of a long table sat a lady belonging to the Society of Friends. She was reading aloud to about sixteen women prisoners, who were engaged in needlework around it. Each wore a clean-looking blue apron and bib, with a ticket having a number on it suspended from her neck by a red tape. They all rose on my entrance, curtsied respectfully, and then at a signal given resumed their seats and employments. Instead of a scowl, leer, or ill-suppressed laugh, I observed upon their countenances an air of self-respect and gravity, a sort of consciousness of their improved character, and the altered position in which they were placed. I afterwards visited the other wards, which were the counterparts of the first."

The efforts of the ladies, which had been at first concentrated upon the convicted, were soon directed also upon the untried. These still continued in a deplorable state, quarrelling and disorderly, bolder and more reckless because they were in doubt as to their future fate. Unhappily the same measure of success did not wait upon the attempt on this side. Many of these women counted upon an early release, and would not take heartily to work, although when they did they were really and essentially improved. Nor could it be expected that the new régime could be established without occasional insubordination and some backsliding. The rules were sometimes broken. Spirits had been introduced more than once; six or seven cases of drunkenness had occurred. But the women were careful not to break out before the ladies; if they swore, it was out of their hearing, and although they still played cards, it was when the ladies' backs were turned. Mrs. Fry told the Parliamentary committee how she expostulated with the women when she found they still gambled, and how she impressed upon them, if it were true that there were cards in the prison, that she should consider it a proof of their regard if they would have the candour and kindness to bring her their packs. By and by a gentle tap came at her door as she sat alone with the matron, and a trembling woman entered to surrender her forbidden cards; another and another followed, till Mrs. Fry had soon five packs of cards in her possession. The culprits fully expected reproof but Mrs. Fry assured them that their fault was fully condoned, and, much to their surprise, rewarded them for their spontaneous good feeling. This reform seems to have been in the ascendant on the whole, and at the end of the first year it was satisfactorily proved to competent judges, the past and present Lord Mayor, the sheriffs, gaolers, and various grand juries, the ordinary, and others, that an extraordinary change for the better had shown itself in the conduct of the females.

The work done in Newgate soon obtained much publicity, to the undoubted and manifest distaste of those who had accomplished it. It was first noticed in the newspapers by the well-known Robert Owen, who adduced it as a proof of the effects of kindness and regular habits. Prison discipline was at this time attracting attention, and Mrs. Fry's labours were very remarkable in this line. Very soon the female side at Newgate became quite a show. Every one of any status in society, every distinguished traveller, all people with high aims or deep feelings, were constrained to visit the prison. Royalty for the first time took an interest in the gaol. The Duke of Gloucester was among the visitors, and was escorted round by Mrs. Fry in person. Another day she was engaged with the Chancellor of the Exchequer; on a third with the Home Secretary and the Speaker of the House of Commons. Still higher and more public honour was done to this noble woman by the Marquis of Lansdowne in the House of Lords, who in 1818, in a moving address on the state of the English prisons, spoke in terms of the highest eulogy of what had been effected by Mrs. Fry and other benevolent persons in Newgate. After this, admission to view the interior of Newgate was eagerly sought by numbers of persons whose applications could not well be refused, in spite of the inconvenience occasioned by thus turning a place of durance into a sentimental lounge. A more desirable and useful result of these ministrations was the eagerness they bred in others to imitate this noble example. Numbers of persons wrote to Mrs. Fry from all parts of the country, seeking advice and encouragement as to the formation of similar societies. Even magistrates appealed to her regarding the management of their prisons. In consequence of the numerous communications received by the Newgate Association, a "corresponding committee" was formed to give information and send replies. Letters came from various capitals of Europe, including St. Petersburgh, Turin, and Amsterdam, which announced the formation of Ladies' Societies for prison visiting.

During many years following its inauguration, the "Ladies' Association" continued their benevolent exertions with marked and well-deserved success. They did not confine their labours to Newgate, but were equally active in the other metropolitan prisons. They also made the female transports their peculiar charge, and obtained many reforms and ameliorations in the arrangement of the convict ships, and the provision for the women on landing at the Antipodes. That the first brilliant successes should be long and continuously maintained could hardly be expected. As time passed and improvements were introduced, there was not the same room for active intervention, and it was difficult to keep alive the early fire. The energy of the Ladies' Committee, although undiminished, came later on to be occasionally misapplied.

FOOTNOTES:

[135:1] The Philanthropic Society is identical with the Farm School at Redhill, in Surrey, one of the most prosperous and best-managed reformatory schools at the present date. Mr. William Crawfurd, afterwards one of the first inspectors of prisons, was long an active member of the committee during the early days of the Society.

[143:1] This was the germ of the Ladies' Committee, which existed down to 1878.

CHAPTER VI
THE BEGINNING OF PRISON REFORM

Prison reform generally taken up—Mr. Neild's visitation—Howard's great work repeated—Prison Discipline Society formed in 1817—Its distinguished members—The society animadverts upon condition of various prisons—A few brilliant exceptions—Newgate still a byword—Opponents of reform—Sydney Smith laughs at efforts of Prison Discipline Society—Prisoners' treatment—Scenes of horror in Newgate—Serious affrays in the wards—Extra and luxurious food admitted—Ladies' Association—No real separation of the sexes—The Governor, Mr. Cope, an offender in this respect—The press-yard the worst of all—Brutal behaviour of many of those sentenced to death—Criminal lunatics allowed to remain in Newgate—House of Commons' prisoners monopolize hospital and best accommodation in the gaol.

While Elizabeth Fry was engaged upon her self-imposed task in Newgate, other earnest people, inspired doubtless by her noble example, were stirred up to activity in the same great work. It began to be understood that prison reform could only be compassed by continuous and combined effort. The pleadings, however eloquent, of a single individual were unable to more than partially remedy the widespread and colossal evils of British prisons. Howard's energy and devotion were rewarded by lively sympathy, but the desire to improve which followed his exposures was short-lived, and powerless to cope with the persistent neglect of those intrusted with prison management. Twenty-five years later, Mr. Neild, a second Howard, and as indefatigable and self-sacrificing, found by personal visitation that the condition of gaols throughout the kingdom was, with a few bright exceptions, still deplorable and disgraceful. Mr. Neild was compelled to admit in 1812 that "the great reformation produced by Howard was in several places merely temporary: certain prisons which had been ameliorated under the persuasive influence of his kind advice were relapsing into their former horrid state of privation, filthiness, severity, or neglect; many new dungeons had aggravated the evils against which his sagacity could not but remonstrate; the motives for a transient amendment were becoming paralyzed, and the effect had ceased with the cause."

It was in 1817 that a small band of philanthropists resolved to form themselves into an association for the improvement of prison discipline. They were hopeless of any general reform by the action of the executive alone. They felt that private enterprise might with advantage step in, and by the collection and diffusion of information, and the reiteration of sound advice, greatly assist the good work. The association was organized under the most promising auspices. A king's son, the Duke of Gloucester, was the patron; among the vice-presidents were many great peers of the realm, several bishops, and a number of members of the House of Commons, including Mr. Manners Sutton, Mr. Sturges Bourne, Sir James Mackintosh, Sir James Scarlett, and William Wilberforce. An active committee was appointed, comprising many names already well known, some of them destined to become famous in the annals of philanthropy. One of the moving spirits was the Honourable H. G. Bennet, M. P., whose vigorous protests against the lamentable condition of Newgate have already been recorded. Mrs. Fry's brother, Mr. Samuel Hoare, Junior, was chairman of the committee, on which also served many noted members of the Society of Friends—Mr. Gurney, Mr. Fry, Messrs. Forster, and Mr. T. F. Buxton, the coadjutor of Wilberforce in the great anti-slavery struggle. Mr. Buxton had already been associated with Mrs. Fry in the Newgate visitation, and his attention had thus been drawn to the neglected state of English prisons. These gentlemen formed the famous English Prison Discipline Society and laboured strenuously and unceasingly in their efforts to ameliorate the condition of English prisons. They found everywhere a crying need for reform, although here and there were a few brilliant exceptions to this cruel, callous neglect. Already, as early as 1818, a prison existed at Bury St. Edmunds which was a model for imitation to others at that time, and which even fulfilled many of the exacting requirements of modern days. The great principles of classification, cleanliness, and employment were closely observed. There were eighty-four separate sleeping-cells, and unless the gaol was overcrowded, every inmate passed the night alone, and in comparative comfort, with a bed and proper bedding. The prison stood on a dry, airy situation outside the town. Prisoners on reception were treated as they are now-a-days—bathed, dressed in prison clothes, and inspected by the surgeon. No irons were worn except as a punishment. Personal cleanliness was insisted upon, and all parts of the prison were kept scrupulously clean. There was an infirmary, properly found and duly looked after. No idleness was permitted among the inmates. Trades were taught, or prisoners were allowed to follow their own if suitable. There was, besides, a mill for grinding corn, somewhat similar to a turn-spit, which prisoners turned by walking in rows. This made exertion compulsory, and imposed hard labour as a proper punishment. Another gaol, that of Ilchester, was also worthy of all commendation. It exhibited all the good points of that at Bury. At Ilchester the rule of employment had been carried further. A system not adopted generally till nearly half a century later had already prevailed at Ilchester. The new gaol had been in a great measure constructed by the prisoners themselves. Masons, bricklayers, carpenters, painters had been employed upon the buildings, and the work was pronounced excellent by competent judges. Industrial labour had also been introduced with satisfactory results. Blanket weaving and cloth spinning were carried on prosperously, and all the material for prisoners' apparel was manufactured in the gaol. There were work-rooms for wool-washing, dyeing, carding, and spinning. The looms were constantly busy. Tailors were always at work, and every article of clothing and bedding was made up within the walls. There was a prison laundry too, where all the prisoners' linen was regularly washed. The moral welfare of the inmates was as closely looked after as the physical. There was an attentive chaplain, a schoolmaster, and regular instruction.

Compared with the last mentioned institutions Newgate compared unfavourably. Its evils were inherent and irremediable, and the need for reform was imperative, yet there were those who, wedded to ancient ideas, were intolerant of change, and they would not admit the existence of any evils. One smug alderman, a member of the House of Commons, sneered at the ultra philanthropy of the champions of prison improvement. Speaking in a debate on prison matters, he declared that "our prisoners have all that prisoners ought to have, without gentlemen think they ought to be indulged with Turkey carpets." The Society for the Improvement of Prison Discipline was taxed with a desire to introduce a system tending to divest punishment of its just and salutary terrors; an imputation which the Society indignantly and very justly repudiated, the statement being, as they said, "refuted by abundant evidence, and having no foundation whatever in truth."

Among those whom the Society found arrayed against it was Sydney Smith, who, in a caustic article contributed to the "Edinburgh Review," protested against the pampering of criminals. While fully admitting the good intentions of the Society, he condemned their ultra humanitarianism as misplaced. He took exceptions to various of the proposals of the Society. He thought they tended too much toward a system of indulgence and education in gaols. He objected to the instruction of prisoners in reading and writing. "A poor man who is lucky enough," he said, "to have his son committed for a felony educates him under such a system for nothing, while the virtuous simpleton who is on the other side of the wall is paying by the quarter for these attainments." He was altogether against too liberal a diet; he disapproved of industrial occupations in gaols, as not calculated to render prisons terrible. "There should be no tea and sugar, no assemblage of female felons around the washing-tub, nothing but beating hemp and pulling oakum and pounding bricks—no work but what was tedious, unusual. . . . In prisons, which are really meant to keep the multitude in order, and to be a terror to evil-doers, there must be no sharings of profits, no visiting of friends, no education but religious education, no freedom of diet, no weavers' looms or carpenters' benches. There must be a great deal of solitude, coarse food, a dress of shame, hard, incessant, irksome, eternal labour, a planned and regulated and unrelenting exclusion of happiness and comfort."

Undeterred by these sarcasms and misrepresentations, the Society pursued its laudable undertaking with remarkable energy and great singleness of purpose. After a few years of active exertion legislation was obtained to enforce the needful change, but still Newgate continued a bye-word. Some reforms had certainly been introduced, such as the abolition of irons, already referred to, and the establishment of male and female infirmaries. The regular daily visitation of the chaplain was also insisted upon. But it was pointed out in 1823 that defective construction must always bar the way to any radical improvement in Newgate. Without enlargement no material change in discipline or interior economy could possibly be introduced. The chapel still continued incommodious and insufficient; female prisoners were still exposed to the full view of the males, the netting in front of the gallery being perfectly useless as a screen. In 1824 Newgate had no glass in its windows, except in the infirmary and one ward of the chapel yard; and the panes were filled in with oiled paper, an insufficient protection against the weather; and as the window-frames would not shut tight, the prisoners complained much of the cold, especially at night. In 1827 the Society was compelled to report that "no material change had taken place in Newgate since the passing of the prison laws of 1823-4, and that consequently the observance of their most important provisions was habitually neglected."

And so it went on—the same old story—evil constantly in the ascendant, the least criminal at the mercy of the most depraved. Under the reckless contempt for regulations, the apathy of the authorities, and the undue prominence of those who, as convicted felons, should have been most sternly repressed, the most hardened and the oldest in vice had the best of it, while the inexperienced beginner went to the wall. Edward Gibbon Wakefield, who spent three years in Newgate from 1835, said with justice that incredible scenes of horror occurred there. It was, in his opinion, the greatest nursery of crime in London. The days were passed in idleness, debauchery, riotous quarrelling, immoral conversation, gambling, in direct contravention of parliamentary rules, instruction in all nefarious processes, lively discourse upon past criminal exploits, elaborate discussion of others to be perpetrated after release. No provision whatever was made for the employment of prisoners, no materials were purchased, no trade instructors appointed. There was no school for adults; only the boys were taught anything, and their instructor, with his assistant, were convicted prisoners. Idle hands and unoccupied brains found in mischief the only means of whiling away the long hours of incarceration. Gaming of all kinds, although forbidden by the Gaol Acts, was habitually practised. This was admitted in evidence by the turnkeys, and was proved by the appearance of the prison tables, which bore the marks of gaming-boards deeply cut into them. Prisoners confessed that it was a favourite occupation, the chief games being "shoving halfpence" on the table, pitch in the hole, cribbage, dominoes, and common tossing, at which as much as four or five shillings would change hands in an hour.

But this was not the only amusement. Most of the wards took in the daily papers, the most popular being the "Times," "Morning Herald," and "Morning Chronicle;" on Sunday the "Weekly Dispatch," "Bell's Life," and the "Weekly Messenger." The newsman had free access to the prison; he passed in unsearched and unexamined, and, unaccompanied by an officer, went at once to his customers, who bought their paper and paid for it themselves. The news-vendor was also a tobacconist, and he had thus ample means of introducing to the prisoners the prohibited but always much-coveted and generally procurable weed. In the same way the wardsman laid in his stock to be retailed. Other light literature besides the daily journals was in circulation: novels, flash songs, play-books, such as "Jane Shore," "Grimm's German Tales," with Cruikshank's illustrations, and publications which in these days would have been made the subject of a criminal prosecution. One of these, published by Stockdale, was stigmatized officially as a book of the most disgusting nature. There was also a good supply of Bibles and prayers, the donation of a philanthropic gentleman, Captain Brown, but these, particularly the Bibles, bore little appearance of having been used. Drink, in more or less unlimited quantities, was still to be had. Spirits certainly were now excluded; but a potman, with full permission of the sheriffs, brought in beer for sale from a neighbouring public-house, and visited all the wards with no other escort than the prisoner gatesman. The quantity to be issued per head was limited by the prison regulations to one pint, but no steps were taken to prevent any prisoner from obtaining more if he could pay for it. The beer-man brought in as much as he pleased; he sold it without the controlling presence of an officer. Not only did prisoners come again and again for a "pint," but large quantities were carried off to the wards to be drunk later in the day.

There were more varied, and at times, especially when beer had circulated freely, more uproarious diversions. Wrestling, in which legs were occasionally broken, was freely indulged in; also such low games as "cobham," leap-frog, puss in the corner, and "fly the garter," for which purpose the rugs were spread out to prevent feet slipping on the floor. Feasting alternated with fighting. The weekly introduction of food, to which I shall presently refer, formed the basis of luxurious banquets, washed down by liquor and enlivened by flash songs and thrilling long-winded descriptions of robberies and other "plants." There was much swearing and bad language, the very worst that could be used, from the first thing in the morning to the last thing at night. New arrivals, especially the innocent and still guileless debutant, were tormented with rude horse-play, and assailed by the most insulting "chaff." If any man presumed to turn in too early he was "toed," that is to say, a string was fastened to his big toe while he was asleep, and he was dragged from off his mat, or his bedclothes were drawn away across the room. The ragged prisoners were very anxious to destroy the clothes of the better dressed, and often lighted small pieces of cloth, which they dropped smouldering into their fellow-prisoners' pockets. Often the victim, goaded to madness, attacked his tormentors; a fight was then certain to follow. These fights sometimes took place in the day-time, when a ring was regularly formed, and two or three stood by the door to watch for the officer's approach. More often they occurred at night, and were continued to the bitter end. The prisoners in this way administered serious punishment on one another. Black eyes and broken noses were always to be seen.

More cruel injuries were common enough, which did not result from honest hand-to-hand fights. The surgeon's journal contained numerous entries of terrible wounds inflicted in a cowardly way. "A serious accident: one of the prisoners had a hot poker run into his eye." "A lad named Matthew White has had a wound in his eye by a bone thrown at him, which very nearly destroyed vision." "There was a disturbance in the transport yard yesterday evening, and the police were called in. During the tumult a prisoner, . . . who was one of the worst of the rioters, was bruised about the head and body." "Watkins' knee-joint is very severely injured." "A prisoner Baxter is in the infirmary in consequence of a severe injury to his wrist-joint." Watkins' case, referred to above, is made the subject of another and a special report from the surgeon. He was in the transport side, when one of his fellows, in endeavouring to strike another prisoner with a large poker, missed his aim, and struck Watkins' knee. . . . Violent inflammation and extensive suppuration ensued, and for a considerable time amputation seemed inevitable. After severe suffering prolonged for many months, the inflammation was subdued, but the cartilage of the knee-joint was destroyed, and he was crippled for life. On another occasion a young man, who was being violently teased, seized a knife and stabbed his tormentor in the back. The prisoner who used the knife was secured, but it was the wardsman, and not the officers, to whom the report was made, and no official inquiry or punishment followed.

Matters were at times still worse, and the rioting went on to such dangerous lengths as to endanger the safety of the building. On one occasion a disturbance was raised which was not quelled until windows had been broken and forms and tables burned. The officers were obliged to go in among the prisoners to restore order with drawn cutlasses, but the presence and authority of the governor himself became indispensable. The worst fights occurred on Sunday afternoons; but nearly every night the act of locking up became, from the consequent removal of all supervision, the signal for the commencement of obscene talk, revelry, and violence.

Other regulations laid down by the Gaol Acts were still defied. One of these was that prisoners should be restricted to the gaol allowance of food; but all could still obtain as much extra, and of a luxurious kind, as their friends chose to bring them in. Visitors were still permitted to come with supplies on given days of the week, about the only limitation being that the food should be cooked, and cold; hot meat, poultry, and fish were forbidden. But the inspectors found in the ward cupboards mince-pies and other pasties, cold joints, hams, and so forth. Many other articles were introduced by visitors, including money, tobacco, pipes, and snuff. From the same source came the two or three strong files found in one ward, together with four bradawls, several large iron spikes, screws, nails, and knives; all of them instruments calculated to facilitate attempts to break out of prison, and capable of becoming most dangerous weapons in the hands of desperate and determined men. The nearly indiscriminate admission of visitors, although restricted to certain days, continued to be an unmixed evil. The untried might see their friends three times a week, the convicted only once. On these occasions precautions were supposed to be taken to exclude bad characters, yet many persons of notoriously loose life continually obtained admittance. Women saw men if they merely pretended to be wives; even boys were visited by their sweethearts. Decency was, however, insured by a line of demarcation, and visitors were kept upon each side of a separated double iron railing. But no search was made to intercept prohibited articles at the gate, and there was no permanent gate-keeper, which would have greatly helped to keep out bad characters. Some idea of the difficulty and inconvenience of these lax regulations as regards visiting, may be gathered from the statement that as many as three hundred were often admitted on the same day—enough to altogether upset what small show of decorum and discipline was still preserved in the prison. Perhaps the worst feature of the visiting system was the permission accorded to male prisoners under the name of husbands, brothers, and sons to have access to the female side on Sundays and Wednesdays, in order to visit their supposed relations there.

On this female side, where the Ladies' Association still reigned supreme, more system and a greater semblance of decorum was maintained. But the separation of the sexes was not rigidly carried out in Newgate as yet. We have seen that male prisoners visited their female relations and friends on the female side. Besides this, the gatesman who prepared the briefs had interviews with female prisoners alone while taking their instructions; a female came alone and unaccompanied by a matron to clean the governor's office in the male prison; male prisoners carried coal into the female prison, when they saw and could speak or pass letters to the female prisoners; and the men could also at any time go for tea, coffee, and sugar to Mrs. Brown's shop, which was inside the female gate. In the bail-dock, where most improper general association was permitted, the female prisoners were often altogether in the charge of male turnkeys. The governor was also personally responsible for gross contravention of this rule of separation, and was in the habit of drawing frequently upon the female prison for prisoners to act as domestic servants in his own private dwelling. Some members of the Ladies' Association observed and commented upon the fact that a young rosy-cheeked girl had been kept by the governor from transportation, while older women in infirm health were sent across the seas. His excuse was that he had given the girl his promise that she should not go, an assumption of prerogative which by no means rested with him; but he afterwards admitted that the girl had been recommended to him by the principal turnkey, who knew something of her friends. This woman was really his servant, employed to help in cleaning, and taken on whenever there was extra work to be done. The governor had a great dislike, he said, to seeing strangers in his house. This girl had been first engaged on account of the extra work entailed by certain prisoners committed by the House of Commons, who had been lodged in the governor's own house. The house at this time was full of men and visitors; waiters came in from the taverns with meals. Some of the prisoners had their valets, and all these were constantly in and out of the kitchen where this female prisoner was employed. There was revelling and roystering, as usual, with "high life below-stairs." The governor sent down wine on festive occasions, of which no doubt the prisoner housemaid had her share. It can hardly be denied that the governor, in his treatment of this woman, was acting in flagrant contravention of all rules.

Bad as were the various parts of the gaol already dealt with, there still remained one where the general callous indifference and mismanagement culminated in cruel and culpable neglect. The condition of the capitally-convicted prisoners after sentence was still very disgraceful. The side they occupied, still known as the press-yard, consisted of two dozen rooms and fifteen cells. In these various chambers, until just before the inspectors made their report, all classes of the condemned, those certain to suffer, and the larger number who were nearly certain of a reprieve, were mingled without discrimination, the old and the young, the murderer and the child who had broken into a dwelling. All privacy was impossible under the circumstances. At times the numbers congregated were very great; as many as fifty or sixty, and even a larger number, were crowded into the press-yard. The better-disposed complained bitterly of what they had to endure; one man declared that the language of the condemned rooms was disgusting, that he was dying a death every day in being compelled to associate with such characters. In the midst of the noisy and blasphemous talk no one could pursue his meditations; and any who tried to pray became the sport and ridicule of his brutal fellows.

Owing to the repeated entreaties of the criminals who could hardly hope to escape the gallows, some show of classification was carried out, and when the inspectors visited Newgate they found the three certain to die in a day-room by themselves; in a second room were fourteen more who had every hope of a reprieve. The whole of these seventeen had, however, a common airing-yard, and took their exercise there at the same time, so that men in the most awful situation, daily expecting to be hanged, were associated continually with a number of those who could look with certainty on a mitigation of punishment. The latter, light-hearted and reckless, conducted themselves in the most unseemly fashion, and with as much indifference as the inmates of the other parts of the prison. They amused themselves after their own fashion; played all day long at blind-man's-buff and leap-frog, or beat each other with a knotted handkerchief, laughing and uproarious, utterly unmindful of the companionship of men upon whom lay the shadow of an impending shameful death. Men whose fate was uncertain, and those most seriously inclined, complained of these annoyances, so subversive of meditation, so disturbing to the thoughts; they suffered sickening anxiety, and wished to be locked up alone. This indiscriminate association lasted for months, during the whole of which time the unhappy convicts who had but little hope of commutation were exposed to the mockery of their reckless associates.

The lax discipline maintained in Newgate was still further deteriorated by the presence of two other classes of prisoners who ought never to have been inmates of such a gaol. One of these were the criminal lunatics, who were at this time and for long previous continuously imprisoned there. As the law stood at that particular time any two of the justices might remove a prisoner found to be insane, either on commitment or arraignment, to an asylum, and the Secretary of State had the same power as regards any who became insane while undergoing sentence. These powers were not invariably put in force, and there were in consequence many unhappy lunatics in Newgate and other gaols, whose proper place was the asylum. At the time the Lords' Committee sat there were eight thus retained in Newgate, and a return in the appendix of the Lords' report gives a total of thirty-nine lunatics confined in various gaols, many of them guilty of murder and other serious crimes. The inspectors in the following year, on examining the facts, found that some of these poor creatures had been in confinement for long periods: at Newgate and York Castle as long as five years; at Ilchester and Morpeth for seven years; at Warwick for eight years, at Buckingham and Hereford for eleven years, at Appleby for thirteen years, at Anglesea for fifteen years, at Exeter for sixteen years, and at Pembroke for no less a period than twenty-four years.

It was manifestly wrong that such persons, visited by the most dreadful of calamities, should be detained in a common prison. Not only did their presence tend greatly to interfere with the discipline of the prison, but their condition was deplorable in the extreme. The lunatic became the sport of the idle and the depraved. His cure was out of the question; he was placed in a situation "beyond all others calculated to confirm his malady and prolong his sufferings." The matter was still further complicated at Newgate by the presence within the walls of sham lunatics. Some of those included in the category had actually been returned as sane from the asylum to which they had been sent, and there was always some uncertainty as to who was mad and who not. Prisoners indeed were known to boast that they had saved their necks by feigning insanity. It was high time that the unsatisfactory state of the law as regards the treatment of criminal lunatics should be remedied, and not the least of the good services rendered by the new inspectors was their inquiry into the status of these unfortunate people, and their recommendation to improve it.

The other inmates of the prison, of an exceptional character, and exempted from the regular discipline, such as it was, were the ten persons committed to Newgate by the House of Commons in 1835. These were the gentlemen concerned in the bribery case at Ipswich in that year.

Many of the old customs once prevalent in the State Side, so properly condemned and abolished, were revived for the convenience of these gentlemen, whose incarceration was thus rendered as little like imprisonment as possible. A certain number, who could afford the high rate of a guinea per diem, fixed by the under sheriff, were lodged in the governor's house, slept there, and had their meals provided for them from the Sessions' House or London Coffee-House. A few others, who could not afford a payment of more than half a guinea, were permitted to monopolize a part of the prison infirmary, where the upper ward was exclusively appropriated to their use. They also had their meals sent in, and, with the food, wine almost *ad libitum*. A prisoner, one of the wardsmen, waited on those in the infirmary; the occupants of the governor's house had their own servants, or those of the governor. As a rule, visitors, many of them persons of good position, came and went all day long, and as late as nine at night; some to the infirmary, many more to the governor's house. There were no restraints, cards and backgammon were played, and the time passed in feasting and revelry. Even Mr. Cope admitted that the committal of this class of prisoners to Newgate was most inconvenient.

Enough has probably been said to give a complete picture of the disgraceful state in which Newgate still remained in the early part of the nineteenth century.

CHAPTER VII
INTERESTING INSTANCES

Description of the new gallows at Newgate—"The fall of the leaf"—Great crowds at the Old Bailey, and as brutal as of old—Enormous crowd at Governor Wall's execution—Execution of Holloway and Haggerty—Terrible loss of life in the crowd—Awful levity displayed—Amelioration of the criminal code—Executions more rare—Capital punishment gradually restricted to murderers—Dissection of the bodies abolished—Public exhibition of bodies also discontinued—Exhibition of the body of Williams, who murdered the Marrs—Hanging in chains given up—Failures at executions—Culprits fight for life—Cases of Charles White, of Luigi Buranelli, of William Bousfield—Calcraft and his method of hanging—Other hangmen—The cost of a hangman.

The discontinuance of the long-practised procession to Tyburn, and the reasons for this change have already been fully set forth. The terrible spectacle was as demoralizing to the public, for whose admonition it was intended, as the exposure was brutal and cruel towards the principal actors. The decision to remove the scene of action to the immediate front of Newgate was in the right direction, as making the performance shorter and diminishing the area of display. But the Old Bailey was not exclusively used; at first, and for some few years after 1784, executions took place occasionally at a distance from Newgate. This was partly due to the survival of the old notion that the scene of the crime ought also to witness the retribution; partly because residents in and about the Old Bailey raised a loud protest against the constant erection of the scaffold in their neighbourhood. As regards the first, I find that in 1786 John Hogan, the murderer of a Mr. Odell, an attorney who resided in Charlotte Street, Rathbone Place, was executed on a gibbet in front of his victim's house. Lawrence Jones, a burglar, was in 1793 ordered for execution in Hatton Garden, near the house he had robbed; and when he evaded the sentence by suicide, his body was exhibited in the same neighbourhood, extended upon a plank on the top of an open cart, in his clothes, and fettered. From 1809 to 1812, Execution Dock, on the banks of the Thames, was still retained. Here John Sutherland, commander of the British armed transport "The Friends," suffered on the 29th June, 1809, for the murder of his cabin-boy, whom he stabbed after much ill-usage on board the ship as it lay in the Tagus. On the 18th December, 1812, two sailors, Charles Palm and Sam Tilling, were hanged at the same place for the murder of their captain, James Keith, of the trading vessel "Adventure," upon the high seas. They were taken in a cart to the place of execution, amidst a vast concourse of people. "Palm, as soon as he was seated in the cart, put a quid of tobacco into his mouth, and offered another to his companion, who refused it with indignation. . . . Some indications of pity were offered for the fate of Tilling; for Palm, execration alone."

But the Old Bailey gradually, and in spite of all objections urged, monopolized the dread business of execution. The first affair of the kind on this spot was on the 3rd of December, 1783, when, in pursuance of an order issued by the Recorder to the sheriffs of Middlesex and the keeper of His Majesty's gaol, Newgate, a scaffold was erected in front of that prison for the execution of several convicts named by the Recorder. "Ten were executed; the scaffold hung with black; and the inhabitants of the neighbourhood, having petitioned the sheriffs to remove the scene of execution to the old place, were told that the plan had been well considered, and would be persevered in." The following 23rd April, it is stated that the malefactors ordered for execution on the 18th inst. were brought out of Newgate about eight in the morning, and suspended on a gallows of a new construction. "After hanging the usual time they were taken down, and the machine cleared away in half-an-hour. By practice the art is much improved, and there is no part of the world in which villains are hanged in so neat a manner, and with so little ceremony."

A full description of this new gallows, which was erected in front of the debtors' door, is to be found in contemporary records. "The criminals are not exposed to view till they mount the fatal stage. The last part of the stage, or that next to the gaol, is enclosed by a temporary roof, under which are placed two seats for the reception of the sheriffs, one on each side of the stairs leading to the scaffold. Round the north, west, and south sides are erected galleries for the reception of officers, attendants, etc., and at the distance of five feet from the same is fixed a strong railing all round the scaffold to enclose a place for the constables. In the middle of this machinery is placed a movable platform, in form of a trap-door, ten feet long by eight wide, on the middle of which is placed the gibbet, extending from the gaol across the Old Bailey. This movable platform is raised six inches higher than the rest of the scaffold, and on it the convicts stand; it is supported by two beams, which are held in their place by bolts. The movement of the lever withdraws the bolts, the platform falls in;" and this, being much more sudden and regular than that of a cart drawn away, had the effect of causing immediate death. A broadsheet dated April 24th, 1787, describing an execution on the newly invented scaffold before the debtors' door, Newgate, says, "The scaffold on which these miserable people suffered is a temporary machine which was drawn out of the yard of the sessions' house by horses; . . . it is supported by strong posts fixed into grooves made in the street; . . . the whole is temporary, being all calculated to take to pieces, which are preserved within the prison."

This contrivance appears to have been copied, with improvements, from that which had been used in Dublin at a still earlier date; for that city claims the priority in establishing the custom of hanging criminals at the gaol itself. The Dublin "engine of death," as the gallows are styled in the account from which the following description is taken, consisted of an iron bar parallel to the prison wall, and about four feet from it, but strongly affixed thereto with iron scroll clamps. "From this bar hang several iron loops, in which the halters are tied. Under this bar at a proper distance is a piece of flooring or platform, projecting somewhat beyond the range of the iron bar, and swinging upon hinges affixed to the wall. The entrance upon this floor or leaf is from the middle window over the gate of the prison; and this floor is supported below, while the criminals stand upon it, by two pieces of timber, which are made to slide in and out of the prison wall through apertures made for that purpose. When the criminals are tied up and prepared for their fate, this floor suddenly falls down, upon withdrawing the supporters inwards. They are both drawn at once by a windlass, and the unhappy culprits remain suspended." This mode of execution, it is alleged, gave rise to the old vulgar chaff, "Take care, or you'll die at the fall of the leaf." The machinery in use in Dublin is much the same as that employed at many gaols now-a-days. But the fall apart and inwards of two leaves is considered superior. The latter is the method still followed at Newgate.

The sentences inflicted in front of Newgate were not limited to hanging. In the few years which elapsed between the establishment of the gallows at Newgate and the abolition of the practice of burning females for petty treason, more than one woman suffered this penalty at the Old Bailey. One case is preserved by Catnach, that of Phœbe Harris, who in 1788 was "barbariously" executed and afterward burned before Newgate for coining. She is described as a well-made little woman, something more than thirty years of age, of a pale complexion and not disagreeable features. "When she came out of prison she appeared languid and terrified, and trembled greatly as she advanced to the stake, where the apparatus for the punishment she was about to experience seemed to strike her mind with horror and consternation, to the exclusion of all power of recollectedness in preparation for the approaching awful moment." She walked from the debtors' door to a stake fixed in the ground about halfway between the scaffold and Newgate Street. She was immediately tied by the neck to an iron bolt fixed near the top of the stake, and after praying fervently for a few minutes, the steps on which she stood were drawn away, and she was left suspended. A chain fastened by nails to the stake was then put round her body by the executioner with his assistants. Two cart-loads of faggots were piled about her, and after she had hung for half-an-hour the fire was kindled. The flames presently burned the halter, the body fell a few inches, and hung then by the iron chain. The fire had not quite burned out at twelve, in nearly four hours, that is to say. A great concourse of people attended on this melancholy occasion.

The change from Tyburn to the Old Bailey had worked no improvement as regards the gathering together of the crowd or its demeanour. As many spectators as ever thronged to see the dreadful show, and they were packed into a more limited space, disporting themselves as heretofore by brutal horseplay, coarse jests, and frantic yells. It was still the custom to offer warm encouragement or bitter disapproval, according to the character and antecedents of the sufferer. The highwayman, whose exploits many in the crowd admired or emulated, was cheered and bidden to die game; the man of better birth could hope for no sympathy, whatever his crime. At the execution of Governor Wall, in 1802, the furious hatred of the mob was plainly apparent in their appalling cries. His appearance on the scaffold was the signal for three prolonged shouts from an innumerable populace, the brutal effusion of one common sentiment. It was said that so large a crowd had never collected since the execution of Mrs. Brownrigg, nor had the public indignation risen so high. Pieman and ballad-monger did their usual roaring trade amidst the dense throng. No sooner was the job finished than half-a-dozen competitors appeared, each offering the identical rope for sale at a shilling an inch. One was the "yeoman of the halter," a Newgate official, the executioner's assistant, whom Mr. J. T. Smith, who was present at the execution, describes as "a most diabolical-looking little wretch—Jack Ketch's head man." The yeoman was, however, undersold by his wife, "Rosy Emma, exuberant in talk and hissing hot from Pie Corner, where she had taken her morning dose of gin-and-bitters." A little further off, says Mr. Smith, was "a lath of a fellow past threescore years and ten, who had just arrived from the purlieus of Black Boy Alley, woebegone as Romeo's apothecary, exclaiming, 'Here's the identical rope at sixpence an inch.'"

Whenever the public attention had been specially called to a particular crime, either on account of its atrocity, the doubtfulness of the issue, or the superior position of the perpetrator, the attendance at the execution was certain to be tumultuous, and the conduct of the mob disorderly. This was notably the case at the execution of Holloway and Haggerty in 1807, an event long remembered from the fatal and disastrous consequences which followed it. They were accused by a confederate, who, goaded by conscience, had turned approver, of the murder of a Mr. Steele, who kept a lavender warehouse in the city, and who had gardens at Feltham, whither he often went to distil the lavender, returning to London the same evening. One night he was missing, and after a long interval his dead body was discovered, shockingly disfigured, in a ditch. Four years passed without the detection of the murderers, but in the beginning of 1807 one of them, at that time just sentenced to transportation, made a full confession, and implicated Holloway and Haggerty. They were accordingly apprehended and brought to trial, the informer, Hanfield by name, being accepted as king's evidence. Conviction followed mainly on his testimony; but the two men, especially Holloway, stoutly maintained their innocence to the last. Very great excitement prevailed in the town throughout the trial, and this greatly increased when the verdict was known.

An enormous crowd assembled to witness the execution, amounting, it was said, to the hitherto unparalleled number of forty thousand. By eight o'clock not an inch of ground in front of the platform was unoccupied. The pressure soon became so frightful that many would have willingly escaped from the crowd; but their attempts only increased the general confusion. Very soon women began to scream with terror; some, especially of low stature, found it difficult to remain standing, and several, although held up for some time by the men nearest them, presently fell, and were at once trampled to death. Cries of Murder! murder! were now raised, and added greatly to the horrors of the scene. Panic became general. More women, children, and many men were borne down, to perish beneath the feet of the rest. The most affecting and distressing scene was at Green Arbour Lane, just opposite the debtors' door of the prison. Here a couple of piemen had been selling their wares; the basket of one of them, which was raised upon a four-legged stool, was upset. The pieman stooped down to pick up his scattered stock, and some of the mob, not seeing what had happened, stumbled over him. No one who fell ever rose again. Among the rest was a woman with an infant at the breast. She was killed, but in the act of falling she forced her child into the arms of a man near her, and implored him in God's name to save it; the man, needing all his care for his own life, threw the child from him, and it passed along the heads of the crowd, to be caught at last by a person who struggled with it to a cart and deposited it there in safety. In another part of the crowd seven persons met their death by suffocation.

In this convulsive struggle for existence people fought fiercely with one another, and the weakest, of course the women, went under. One cart-load of spectators having broken down, some of its occupants fell off the vehicle, and were instantly trampled to death. This went on for more than an hour, until the malefactors were cut down and the gallows removed; then the mob began to thin, and the streets were cleared by the city marshals and a number of constables. The catastrophe exceeded the worst anticipations. Nearly one hundred dead and dying lay about; and after all had been removed, the bodies for identification, the wounded to hospitals, a cart-load of shoes, hats, petticoats, and fragments of wearing apparel were picked up. St. Bartholomew's Hospital was converted into an impromptu morgue, and all persons who had relatives missing were admitted to identify them. Among the dead was a sailor lad whom no one knew; he had his pockets filled with bread and cheese, and it was generally supposed that he had come a long distance to see the fatal show.

A tremendous crowd assembled when Bellingham was executed in 1812 for the murder of Spencer Percival, at that time prime minister; but there were no serious accidents, beyond those caused by the goring of a maddened, over-driven ox which forced its way through the crowd. Precautions had been taken by the erection of barriers, and the posting of placards at all the avenues to the Old Bailey, on which was printed, "Beware of entering the crowd! Remember thirty poor persons were pressed to death by the crowd when Haggerty and Holloway were executed!" The concourse was very great, notwithstanding these warnings. It was still greater at Fauntleroy's execution in 1824, when no less than 100,000 persons assembled, it was said. Every window and roof which could command a view of the horrible performance was occupied. All the avenues and approaches, places whence nothing could be seen of the scaffold, were blocked by persons who had overflowed from the area in front of the gaol.

At Courvoisier's execution in 1840 it was the same, or worse. As early as six o'clock the number assembled already exceeded that seen on ordinary occasions; by seven o'clock the whole space was so thronged that it was impossible to move one way or the other. Some persons were kept for more than five hours standing against the barriers, and many nearly fainted from exhaustion. Every window had its party of occupants; the adjoining roofs were equally crowded. High prices were asked and paid for front seats or good standing room. As much as £5 was given for the attic story of the Lamb's Coffee House; £2 was a common price for a window. At the George public-house to the south of the drop, Sir W. Watkin Wynn, Bart., hired a room for the night and morning, which he and a large party of friends occupied before and during the execution; in an adjoining house, that of an undertaker, was Lord Alfred Paget, also with several friends. Those who had hired apartments spent the night in them, keeping up their courage with liquids and cigars. Numbers of ladies were present, although the public feeling was much against their attendance. One well-dressed woman fell out of a first-floor window on to the shoulders of the crowd below, but neither she nor any one else was greatly hurt. The city authorities had endeavoured to take all precautions against panic and excitement among the crowd, and caused a number of stout additional barriers to be erected in front of the scaffold, and although one of these gave way owing to the extraordinary pressure, no serious accident occurred.

But there is little doubt that as executions became more rare they made more impression on the public mind. Already a strong dislike to the reckless and almost indiscriminate application of the extreme penalty was apparent in all classes, and the mitigation of the criminal code, for which Romilly had so strenuously laboured, was daily more and more of an accomplished fact. In 1832 capital punishment was abolished for forgery, except in cases of forging or altering wills or powers of attorney to transfer stock. Nevertheless, after that date no person was executed for this offence. In the same year capital punishment was further restricted, and ceased to be the legal sentence for coining, sheep or horse stealing, and stealing in a dwelling-house. House-breaking, as distinguished from burglary, was similarly exempted in the following year; next, the offences of returning from transportation, stealing post-office letters, and sacrilege were no longer punishable with death. In 1837 Lord John Russell's Acts swept away a number of capital offences, including cutting and maiming, rick-burning, robbery, burglary, and arson. Within two years the number of persons sentenced to death in England had fallen from four hundred and thirty-eight in 1837 to fifty-six in 1839. Gradually the application of capital punishment became more and more restricted, and was soon the penalty for murder alone. While in London, for instance, in 1829, twenty-four persons had been executed for crimes other than murder, from 1832 to 1844 not a single person had been executed in the metropolis except for this the gravest crime. In 1837 the death penalty was practically limited to murder or attempts to murder, and in 1841 this was accepted as the almost universally established rule. Seven other crimes, however, were still capital by law, and so continued till the passing of the Criminal Consolidation Acts of 1861.

With the amelioration of the criminal code, other cruel concomitants of execution also disappeared. In 1832 the dissection of bodies cut down from the gallows, which had been decreed centuries previous, was abolished; the most recent enactment in force was that which directed the dissection of all bodies of executed murderers, the idea being to intensify the dread of capital punishment. That such dread was not universal or deep-seated may be gathered from the fact that well authenticated cases were known of criminals selling their own bodies to surgeons for dissection. This dissection was performed for Newgate prisoners in Surgeons' Hall, adjoining Newgate, the site of the present Sessions' House of the Old Bailey, and the operation was witnessed by students and a number of curious spectators. Lord Ferrers' body was brought to Surgeons' Hall after execution in his own carriage and six; after the post mortem had been performed, the corpse was exposed to view in a first-floor room.

Pennant speaks of Surgeons' Hall as a handsome building, ornamented with Ionic pilasters, and with a double flight of steps to the first floor. Beneath is a door for the admission of the bodies of murderers and other felons. There were other public dissecting rooms for criminals. One was attached to Hicks' Hall, the Clerkenwell Sessions' House, built out of monies provided by Sir

Baptist Hicks, a wealthy alderman of the reign of James I. Persons were still living in 1855 who had witnessed dissections at Hicks' Hall, and "whom the horrid scene, with the additional effect of some noted criminals hanging on the walls, drove out again sick and faint, as we have heard some relate, and with pale and terrified features, to get a breath of air." The dissection of executed criminals was abolished soon after the discovery of the crime of burking, with the idea that ignominy would no longer attach to an operation which ceased to be compulsory for the most degraded beings; and that executors or persons having lawful possession of the bodies of people who had died friendless, would voluntarily surrender them for the advancement of medical science.

Another brutal practice had nearly disappeared about the time of the abolition of dissection. This was the public exhibition of the body, as was done in the case of Mrs. Phipoe, the murderess, who was executed in front of Newgate in 1798, and her body publicly exhibited in a place built for the purpose in the Old Bailey. About this time we find that the bodies of two murderers, Clench and Mackay, "were publicly exposed in a stable in Little Bridge Street, near Apothecaries' Hall, Surgeons' Hall being let to the lieutenancy of the county for the accommodation of the militia." In 1811 Williams, who murdered the Marrs in Ratcliffe Highway, having committed suicide in gaol to escape hanging, it was determined that a public exhibition should be made of the body through the neighbourhood which had been the scene of the monster's crimes. A long procession was formed, headed by constables, who cleared the way with their staves. Then came the newly-formed horse patrol, with drawn cutlasses, parish officers, peace officers, the high constable of the county of Middlesex on horseback, and then the body of Williams, "extended at full length on an inclined platform erected on the cart, about four feet high at the head, and gradually sloping towards the horse, giving a full view of the body, which was dressed in blue trousers and a blue-and-white striped waistcoat, but without a coat, as when found in the cell. On the left side of the head the fatal mall, and on the right the ripping chisel, with which the murders had been committed, were exposed to view. The countenance of Williams was ghastly in the extreme, and the whole had an appearance too horrible for description." The procession traversed Ratcliffe twice, halting for a quarter of an hour in front of the victims' dwelling, and was accompanied throughout by "an immense concourse of persons, eager to get a sight of the murderer's remains. . . . All the shops in the neighbourhood were shut, and the windows and tops of the houses were crowded with spectators."

Hanging in chains upon the gibbet which had served for the execution, or on another specially erected on some commanding spot, had fallen into disuse by 1832. But there was an attempt to revive it at that date, when the act for dispensing with the dissection of criminals was passed. A clause was inserted to the effect that "the bodies of all prisoners convicted of murder should either be hung in chains, or buried under the gallows on which they had been executed, . . . according to the discretion of the court before whom the prisoners might be tried." The revival of this barbarous practice caused much indignation in certain quarters, but it was actually tried in two provincial towns, Leicester and Durham. At the first-named the exhibition nearly created a tumult, and the body was taken down and buried, but not before the greatest scandal had been caused by the unseemly proceedings of the crowd that flocked to see the sight. A sort of fair was held, gaming-tables were set up, cards were played under the gibbet, to the disturbance of the public peace and the annoyance of all decent people. At Jarrow Stake, where the Durham murderer's body was exposed, there were similar scenes, mingled with compassion for the culprit's family, and a subscription was set on foot for them then and there at the foot of the gibbet. Later on, after dark, some friends of the deceased stole the body and buried it in the sand, and this was the end of hanging in chains. After this a law was passed which prescribed that the bodies of all executed murderers should be buried within the walls of the gaol.

Although these objectionable practices had disappeared, there were still many shocking incidents at executions, owing to the bungling and unskilful way in which the operation was performed. The rope still broke sometimes, although it was not often that the horrid scene at Jersey at the beginning of the century was repeated. There the hangman added his weight to that of the suspended culprit, and having first pulled him sideways, then got upon his shoulders, so that the rope broke. "To the great surprise of all who witnessed this dreadful scene, the poor criminal rose straight upon his feet, with the hangman on his shoulders, and immediately loosened the rope with his fingers." After this the sheriffs sent for another rope, but the spectators interfered, and the man was carried back to gaol. The whole case was referred to the king, and the poor wretch, whose crime had been a military one, was eventually pardoned. A somewhat similar event happened at Chester not long afterwards; the ropes by which two offenders were turned off broke a few inches from their necks. They were taken back to gaol, and were again brought out in the afternoon, by which time fresh and stronger ropes had been procured, and the sentence was properly and completely carried out. Other cases might be quoted, especially that of William Snow, *alias* Sketch, who slipped from the gallows at Exeter and fell to the ground. He soon rose to his feet, and, hearing the sorrowful exclamations of the populace, coolly said, "Good people, do not be hurried; I am not, I can wait."

Similar cases were not wanting as regards the executions before Newgate. Others were not less horrible, although there was no failure of apparatus.

Sometimes the condemned man made a hard fight for life. When Charles White was executed in 1823 for arson, he arranged a handkerchief in such a way that the executioner found a difficulty in pinioning his hands. White managed to keep his wrists asunder, and continued to struggle with the officials for some time. Eventually he was pinioned with a cord in the usual manner. On the scaffold he made a violent attempt to loosen his bonds, and succeeded in getting his hands free. Then with a strong effort he pushed off the white cap, and tried to liberate his neck from the halter, which by this time had been adjusted. The hangman summoned assistance, and with help tied the cap over White's face with a handkerchief. The miserable wretch during the whole of this time was struggling with the most determined violence, to the great horror of the spectators. Still he resisted, and having got from the falling drop to the firm part of the platform, he nearly succeeded in tearing the handkerchief from his eyes. However, the ceremony went forward, and when the signal was given the drop sank. The wretched man did not fall with it, but jumped on to the platform, and seizing the rope with his hands, tried to avoid strangulation. The spectacle was horrible; the convict was half on the platform, half hanging, and the convulsions of his body were appalling. The crowd vociferously yelled their disapproval, and at length the executioner forced the struggling criminal from the platform, so that the rope sustained his whole weight. His face was visible to the whole crowd, and was fearful to behold. Even now his sufferings were not at an end, and his death was not compassed until the executioner terminated his sufferings by hanging on to his legs.

When Luigi Buranelli was executed in 1855, through the improper adjustment of the rope his sufferings were prolonged for five minutes; "his chest heaved, and it was evident that his struggle was a fearful one." A worse case still was that of William Bousfield, who, when awaiting execution for murder, about the same date, had attempted to throw himself upon the fire in his condemned cell. He was in consequence so weak when brought out for execution, that he had to be carried by four men, two supporting his body and two his legs. His wretched, abject condition, seated in a chair under the drop, was such as almost to unnerve the executioner Calcraft, who had been further upset by a letter threatening to shoot him when he appeared to perform his task. Calcraft, the moment he had adjusted the cap and rope, ran down the steps, drew the bolt, and disappeared. "For a second or two the body hung motionless, then, with a strength that astonished the attendant officials, Bousfield slowly drew himself up, and rested with his feet on the right side of the drop. One of the turnkeys rushed forward and pushed him off. Again the wretched creature succeeded in obtaining foothold, but this time on the left side of the drop." Calcraft was forced to return, and he once more pushed Bousfield off, who for the fourth time regained his foothold.

Again he was repelled, this time Calcraft adding his weight to the body, and the strangulation was completed.

It was stated in evidence before the Commission on Capital Punishment in 1864, that Calcraft's method of hanging was very rough, much the same as if he had been hanging a dog. Calcraft, of whom mention has just been made, was by trade a lady's shoemaker, and before he took to hanging he was employed as a watchman at Reid's brewery in Liquorpond Street. He was at first engaged as assistant to the executioner Tom Cheshire, but in due course rose to be chief. He was always known as a mild-mannered man of simple tastes, much given to angling in the New River, and a devoted rabbit fancier. He was well known in the neighbourhood where he resided, and the street gamins cried "Jack Ketch" as he went along the street. While Calcraft was in office other aspirants to fame appeared in the field. One was Askern, who had been a convicted prisoner at York, but who consented to act as hangman when Calcraft was otherwise engaged and no other functionary could be obtained. It was not always easy to hire a hangman. There is still extant a curious petition presented to the Treasury by Ralph Griffith, Esq., high sheriff of Flintshire, which sets forth that the petitioner had been at great expense by sending clerks and agents to Liverpool and Shrewsbury to hire an executioner. The man to be hanged belonged to Wales, and no Welshman would do the job. Travelling expenses of these agents cost £15, and another £10 were spent in the hire of a Shropshire man, who deserted, and was pursued, but without success. Another man was hired, himself a convict, whose fees for self and wife were twelve guineas. Then came the cost of the gallows, £4. 12*s.*; and finally the funeral, cart, coffin, and other petty expenses, amounting to £7. 10*s.*, making nearly £50 as the total expense.

CHAPTER VIII
NEWGATE NOTORIETIES

Diminution in certain kinds of crime—Fewer street robberies—Corresponding increase in cases of fraud, forgeries, jewel and bullion robberies—Great commercial frauds—Offences against the person confined to murder and manslaughter—The Cato Street conspiracy—Thistlewood's history—Discovery of the plot—The conspirators' plan and its overthrow—Their trial and execution at the Old Bailey—Attacks on the sovereign—Oxford fires at Queen Victoria—Celebrated frauds and forgeries—Fauntleroy—The last execution for forgery—Joseph Hunton the Quaker—Sir Robert Peel's bill to amend forgery laws—The Forgery Act—Latest cases of abduction—Edward Gibbon Wakefield and Miss Turner—The most remarkable murders of the epoch—Thurtell, Hunt, and Probert kill Mr. Weare—Burke and Hall—Their imitators, Bishop and Williams, in London—Greenacre and Mrs. Gale murder Hannah Brown—Horrible means of disposing of the corpse—Detection, trial, and sentence—Courvoisier murders his master—An epidemic of murder.

The record of crime has been brought down to the second decade of the last century. Some space should be devoted to criminal occurrences of a more recent date, only premising that as accounts become more voluminous I shall be compelled to deal with fewer cases, taking in preference those which are typical and invested with peculiar interest. It is somewhat remarkable that a marked change soon comes over the Calendar. Certain crimes, those against the person especially, diminished gradually. They became less easy or remunerative. Police protection was better and more effective; the streets of London were well lighted, the suburbs were more populous and regularly patrolled. People, moreover, were getting into the habit of carrying but little cash about them, and no valuables but their watches or personal jewelry. Street robberies offered fewer inducements to depredators, and evil-doers were compelled to adopt other methods of preying upon their fellows. This led to a rapid and marked increase in all kinds of fraud; and prominent in the criminal annals of Newgate in these later years will be found numerous remarkable instances of this class of offence—forgeries committed systematically, and for long periods, as in the case of Fauntleroy, to cover enormous defalcations; the fabrication of deeds, wills, and false securities for the purpose of misappropriating funds or feloniously obtaining cash; thefts of bullion, bank-notes, specie, and gold-dust, planned with consummate ingenuity, eluding the keenest vigilance, and carried out with reckless daring; jewel-boxes cleverly stolen under the very noses of owners or care-takers. As time passed, the extraordinary extension of all commercial operations led to many entirely novel and often gigantic financial frauds. The credulity of investors, the unscrupulous dishonesty of bankers, the slackness of supervision over wholly irresponsible agents, produced many terrible monetary catastrophes, and lodged men like Cole, Robson, and Redpath in Newgate.

While the varying conditions of social life thus brought about many changes in the character of offences against property, those against the person became more and more limited to the most heinous, or those which menaced or destroyed life. There was no increase in murder or manslaughter; the number of such crimes remained proportionate to the population. Nor did the methods by which they were perpetrated greatly vary from those in times past. The causes also continued much the same. Passion, revenge, cupidity, sudden ebullitions of homicidal rage, the cold-blooded, calculating atrocity born of self-interest, were still the irresistible incentives to kill. The brutal ferocity of the wild beast once aroused, the same means, the same weapons were employed to do the dreadful deed, the same and happily often futile precautions taken to conceal the crime. Pegsworth, and Greenacre, and Daniel Good merely reproduced types that had gone before, and that have since reappeared. Esther Hibner was as inhuman in her ill-usage of the parish apprentice whom she killed as Martha Brownrigg had been. Thurtell and Hunt followed in the footsteps of Billings, Wood, and Catherine Hayes. Courvoisier might have lived a century earlier. Hocker was found upon the scene of his crime, irresistibly attracted thither, as was Theodore Gardelle. Now and again there seemed to be a recurrence of a murder epidemic, as there had been before; as in the year 1849, a year memorable for the Rush murders at Norwich, the Gleeson Wilson murder at Liverpool, that of the Mannings in London, and of many more. Men like Mobbs, the miscreant known as "General Haynau" on account of his blood-thirstiness, still murdered their wives; or struck in blind rage like Cannon the chimney-sweeper, who savagely killed the policeman.

But at various dates treason distinct and tangible still came to the front: direct attempts to levy war against the State. The well-known Cato Street conspiracy, which grew out of disturbed social conditions after the last French war, amidst general distress, and when the people were beginning to agitate for a larger share of political power, was among the earliest, and to some extent the most desperate, of these. Its ringleaders, Thistlewood and the rest, were after capture honoured by committal as State prisoners to the Tower, but they came one and all to Newgate for trial at the Old Bailey, and remained there after conviction till they were hanged. Later on, the Chartists agitated persistently for the concessions embraced in the so-called People's Charter, many of which are, by more legitimate efforts, engrafted upon the Constitution. But the Chartists sought their ends by riot and rebellion, and gained only imprisonment for their pains. Some five hundred in all were arrested, but only three of these were lodged in Newgate.

The Cato Street conspiracy would have been simply ridiculous but for the recklessness of the desperadoes who planned it. That some thirty or more needy men should hope to revolutionize England is a sufficient proof of the absurdity of their attempt. But they proceeded in all seriousness, and would have shrunk from no outrage or atrocity in furtherance of their foolhardy enterprise. The massacre of the whole of the Cabinet Ministers at one stroke was to be followed by an attack upon "the old man and the old woman," as they styled the Mansion House and the Bank of England. At the former the "Provisional Government" was to be established, which under Thistlewood as dictator was to rule the nation by first handing over its capital to fire and pillage. This Thistlewood had seen many vicissitudes throughout his strange, adventurous career. The son of a respectable Lincolnshire farmer, he became a militia officer, and married a woman with £10,000, in which, however, she had only a life interest. She died early, and Thistlewood, left to his own resources, followed the profession of arms, first in the British service, and then in that of the French revolutionary Government. It was during this period that he was said to have imbibed his revolutionary ideas. Returning to England, he found himself rich in a small landed property, which he presently sold to a man who became bankrupt before he had paid over the purchase money. After this he tried farming, but failed. He married again and came to London, where he soon became notorious as a reckless gambler and a politician holding the most extreme views. In this way he formed the acquaintance of Watson and others, with whom he was arraigned for treasonable practices, and imprisoned. On his release he sent a challenge to Lord Sidmouth, the Home Secretary, and was again arrested and imprisoned. On his second release, goaded by his fancied wrongs, he began to plot a dark and dreadful revenge, and thus the conspiracy in which he was the prime mover took shape, and came to a head.

The Government obtained early and full information of the nefarious scheme. One of the conspirators, by name Edwards, made a voluntary confession to Sir Herbert Taylor one morning at Windsor; after which Thistlewood and his accomplices were closely watched, and measures taken to arrest them when their plans were so far developed that no doubt could remain as to their guilt. The day appointed for the murder and rising actually arrived before the authorities interfered. It was the day on which Lord Harrowby was to entertain his colleagues at dinner in Grosvenor Square. The occasion was considered excellent by the conspirators for disposal of the whole Cabinet at one blow, and it was arranged that one of their number should knock at Lord Harrowby's door on the pretence of leaving a parcel, and that when it was opened the whole band should rush in. While a few secured the servants, the rest were to fall upon Lord Harrowby and his guests. Hand-grenades were to be thrown into the dining-room, and during the noise and confusion the assassination of the ministers was to be completed, the heads of Lord Castlereagh and Lord Sidmouth being carried away in a bag. Lord Harrowby's dinner-party was postponed, but the conspirators knew nothing of it, and those who watched his house were further encouraged in their mistake by the arrival of many carriages, bound, as it happened, to the Archbishop of York's. Meanwhile the main body remained at their headquarters, a ruined stable in Cato Street, Edgeware Road, completing their dispositions for assuming supreme power after the blow had been struck. Here they were surprised by the police, headed by a magistrate, and supported by a strong detachment of Her Majesty's Guards. The police were the first to arrive on the spot, the Guards having entered the street at the wrong end. The conspirators were in a loft, approached by a ladder and a trap-door, access through which could only be obtained one by one. The first constable who entered Thistlewood ran through the body with a sword, but others quickly followed, the lights were extinguished, and a desperate conflict ensued. The Guards, headed by Lord Frederick Fitz Clarence, now reinforced the police, and the conspirators gave way. Nine of the latter were captured, with all the war material, cutlasses, pistols, hand grenades, and ammunition. Thistlewood and fourteen more succeeded for the moment in making their escape, but most of them were subsequently taken. Thistlewood was discovered next morning in a mean house in White Street, Moorfields. He was in bed with his breeches on (in the pockets of which were found a number of cartridges), the black belt he had worn at Cato Street, and a military sash.

The trial of the conspirators came on some six weeks later, at the Old Bailey. Thistlewood made a long and rambling defence, the chief features of which were abuse of Lord Sidmouth, and the vilification of the informer Edwards. Several of the other prisoners took the same line as regards Edwards, and there seems to have been good reason for supposing that he was a greater villain than any of those arraigned. He had been in a state of abject misery, and when he first joined "the reformers," as the Cato Street conspirators called themselves, he had neither a bed to lie upon nor a coat to his back. His sudden access to means unlimited was no doubt due to the profitable *rôle* he soon adopted of Government informer and spy, and it is pretty certain that for some time he served both sides; on the one inveigling silly enthusiasts to join in the plot, and denouncing them on the other. The employment of Edwards, and the manner in which the conspirators were allowed to commit themselves further and further before the law was set in motion against them, were not altogether creditable to the Government. It was asserted, not without foundation, at these trials, that Edwards repeatedly incited the associates he was betraying to commit outrage, to set fire to houses, and throw hand-grenades into the carriages of ministers; that he was, to use Thistlewood's words, "a contriver, instigator, and entrapper." The Government were probably not proud of their agent, for Edwards, after the conviction had been assured, went abroad to enjoy, it was said, an ample pension, so long as he did not return to England.

Five of the conspirators, Thistlewood, Ings, Brunt, Davidson, and Tidd, were sentenced to death, and suffered in the usual way in front of Newgate, with the additional penalty of decapitation, as traitors, after they had been hanged. A crowd as great as any known collected in the Old Bailey to see the ceremony, about which there were some peculiar features worth recording. The reckless demeanour of all the convicts except Davidson was most marked. Thistlewood and Ings sucked oranges on the scaffold; they with Brunt and Tidd scorned the ordinary's ministrations, but Ings said he hoped God would be more merciful to him than men had been. Ings was especially defiant. He sought to cheer Davidson, who seemed affected, crying out, "Come, old cock-of-wax, it will soon be over." As the executioner fastened the noose, he nodded to a friend he saw in the crowd; and catching sight of the coffins ranged around the gallows, he smiled at the show with contemptuous indifference. He roared out snatches of a song about Death or Liberty, and just before he was turned off, yelled out three cheers to the populace whom he faced.

Attacks upon the sovereign were not uncommon after the accession of the young Queen Victoria to the English throne in 1838. It was a form of high treason not unknown in earlier reigns. In 1786 a mad woman, Margaret Nicholson, tried to stab George III as he was alighting from his carriage at the gate of St. James's Palace. She was seized before she could do any mischief, and eventually lodged in Bethlehem Hospital, where she died after forty years' detention, at the advanced age of one hundred. Again, a soldier, by name Hatfield, who had been wounded in the head, and discharged from the army for unsoundness of mind in 1800, fired a pistol at George III from the pit of Drury Lane theatre. William IV was also the victim of a murderous outrage on Ascot racecourse in 1832, when John Collins, "a person in the garb of a sailor, of wretched appearance, and having a wooden leg," threw a stone at the king, which hit him on the forehead, but did no serious injury. Collins, when charged, pleaded that he had lost his leg in action, that he had petitioned without success for a pension, and that, as he was starving, he had resolved on this desperate deed, feeling, as he said, that he might as well be shot or hanged as remain in such a state. He was eventually sentenced to death, but the plea of lunacy was allowed, and he was confined for life.

None of the foregoing attempts were, however, so dastardly or determined as that made by Oxford upon Queen Victoria two years after she ascended the throne. The cowardly crime was probably encouraged by the fearless and confiding manner in which the Queen, secure as it seemed in the affections of her loyal people, freely appeared in public. Oxford, who was only nineteen at the time his offence was committed, had been born at Birmingham, but he came as a lad to London, and took service as a pot-boy to a publican. From this he was promoted to barman, and as such had charge of the business in various public-houses. He left his last situation in April, 1840, and established himself in lodgings in Lambeth, after which he devoted himself to pistol practice in shooting-galleries, sometimes in Leicester Square, sometimes in the Strand, or the West End. His acquaintances often asked his object in this, but he kept his own counsel till the 10th of June. On that day Oxford was on the watch at Buckingham Palace. He saw Prince Albert return there from a visit to Woolwich, and then passed on to Constitution Hill, there to wait until four o'clock in the afternoon, the time at which the Queen and Prince Consort usually took an afternoon drive. About six o'clock, the royal carriage, a low open vehicle drawn by four horses, ridden by postilions, left the palace. Oxford, who had been pacing backwards and forwards with his hands under the lapels of his coat, saw the carriage approach. He was on the right or north side of the road. Prince Albert occupied the same side of the carriage, the Queen the left. As the carriage came up to him Oxford turned, put his hand into his breast, drew a pistol, and fired at the Queen.

The shot missed, and as the carriage passed on, Oxford drew a second pistol and fired again. The Queen saw this second movement, and stooped to avoid the shot; the Prince too rose to shield her with his person. Again, providentially, the bullet went wide of the mark, and the royal party drove back to Clarence House, the Queen being anxious to give the first news of the outrage and of her safety to her mother, the Duchess of Kent. Meanwhile the pistol-shots had attracted the attention of the bystanders, of whom there was a fair collection, as usual, waiting to see the Queen pass. Oxford was seized by a person named Lowe, who was at first mistaken for the assailant. But Oxford at once assumed the responsibility for his crime, saying, "It was I. I did it. I'll give myself up. There is no occasion to use violence. I will go with you." He was taken into custody, and removed first to a police cell, thence committed to Newgate, after he had been examined before the Privy Council. Oxford expressed little anxiety or concern. He asked more than once whether the Queen was hurt, and acknowledged that the pistols were loaded with ball.

A craze for notoriety, to be achieved at any cost, was the one absorbing idea in young Oxford's disordered brain. After his arrest he thought only of the excitement his attempt had raised, nothing of its atrocity, or of the fatal consequences which might have ensued. When brought to trial he hardly realized his position, but gazed with complacency around the crowded court, and eagerly inquired what persons of distinction were present. He smiled continually, and when the indictment was read, burst into loud and discordant fits of laughter. These antics may have been assumed to bear out the plea of insanity set up in his defence, but that there was madness in his family, and that he himself was of unsound mind, could not be well denied. His father, it was proved, had been at times quite mad; and Oxford's mental state might be inferred from his own proceedings and demeanour in court. The whole of the evidence pointed so strongly towards insanity, that the jury brought in a verdict of acquittal on that ground, and Oxford was ordered to be detained during Her Majesty's pleasure. He went from Newgate first to Bethlehem, from which he was removed to Broadmoor on the opening of the great criminal lunatic asylum at that place. He was released from Broadmoor in 1878, and went abroad.

Referring again to the increase of bank forgeries, at one session of the Old Bailey, in 1821, no less than thirty-five true bills were found for passing forged notes. But there were other notorious cases of forgery. That of Fauntleroy the banker, in 1824, caused much excitement at the time on account of the magnitude of the fraud, and the seeming probity of the culprit. Mr. Fauntleroy was a member of a banking firm, which his father had established in conjunction with a gentleman of the name of Marsh, and others. He had entered the house as clerk in 1800; in 1807, when only twenty-two years of age, he succeeded to his father's share in the business. According to Fauntleroy's own case, he found at once that the firm was heavily involved, through advances made to various builders, and that it could only maintain its credit by wholesale discounting. Its embarrassments were greatly increased by the bankruptcy of two of its clients in the building trade, and the bank became liable for a sum of £170,000. New liabilities were incurred to the extent of £100,000 by more failures, and in 1819, by the death of one of the partners, a large sum in cash had to be withdrawn from the bank to pay his heirs. "During these numerous and trying difficulties," says Mr. Fauntleroy, "the house was nearly without resources, and the whole burthen of management falling on me, . . . I sought resources where I could;" in other words, he forged powers of attorney and proceeded to realize securities lodged in his bank under various names. Among the prisoner's private papers, one was found giving full details of the stock he had feloniously sold out, the sum amounting to some £170,000, with a declaration in his own handwriting to the following effect: "In order to keep up the credit of our house, I have forged powers of attorney for the above sums and parties, and sold out to the amount here stated, and without the knowledge of my partners. I kept up the payments of the dividends, but made no entries of such payments in my books. The bank began first to refuse our acceptances, and to destroy the credit of our house; the bank shall smart for it."

Many stories were in circulation at the time of Fauntleroy's trial with regard to his forgeries. It was said that he had by means of them sold out so large an amount of stock, that he paid £16,000 a year in dividends to escape detection. Once he ran a narrow risk of being found out. A lady in the country, who had £13,000 in the stocks, desired her London agent to sell them out. He went to the bank, and found that no stocks stood in her name. He called at once upon Fauntleroy, his client's banker, for an explanation, and was told by Mr. Fauntleroy that the lady had desired *him* to sell out, "which I have done," added the fraudulent banker, "and here are the proceeds," whereupon he produced exchequer bills to the amount. Nothing more was heard of the affair, although the lady declared that she had never instructed Fauntleroy to sell. On another occasion the banker forged a gentleman's name while the latter was sitting with him in his private room, and took the instrument out to a clerk with the ink not dry. It must be added that the Bank of England, on discovering the forgeries, replaced the stock in the names of the original holders, who might otherwise have been completely ruined. A newspaper report of the time describes Fauntleroy "as a well-made man of middle stature. His hair, though gray, was thick, and lay smooth over his forehead. His countenance had an expression of most subdued resignation. The impression which his appearance altogether was calculated to make was that of the profoundest commiseration."

The crime, long carried on without detection, was first discovered in 1820, when it was found that a sum of $10,000, standing in the name of three trustees, of whom Fauntleroy was one, had been sold out under a forged power of attorney. Further investigations brought other similar frauds to light, and fixed the whole sum misappropriated at £170,000, the first forgery dating back to 1814. A run upon the bank immediately followed, which was only met by a suspension of payment and the closing of its doors. Meanwhile public gossip was busy with Fauntleroy's name, and it was openly stated in the press and in conversation that the proceeds of these frauds had been squandered in dissipation, gambling, and debauchery. Fauntleroy was scouted as a licentious libertine, a deep and determined gamester, a spendthrift whose extravagance knew no bounds. It was said that the dinners he gave were of the most sumptuous and *recherché* description. The story goes that one of his most intimate friends, who attended him to the scaffold, entreated him, as on the brink of the grave, and unable to take anything out of the world with him, to reveal the secret of where some wonderful curaçoa was obtained, for which Fauntleroy's cellar was famous. The veil was lifted from his private life, and he was accused of persistent immorality. In his defence he sought to rebut these charges, which indeed were never clearly made out, and it is pretty certain that his own account of the causes which led him into dishonesty was substantially true. He called many witnesses, seventeen in all, to speak of him as they had found him; and these, all respectable city merchants and business men, declared that they had hitherto formed a high opinion of his honour, integrity, and goodness of disposition, deeming him the last person capable of a dishonourable action.

These arguments availed little with the jury, who after a short deliberation found Fauntleroy guilty, and he was sentenced to death. Every endeavour was used, however, to obtain a commutation of sentence. His case was twice argued before the judges on points of law, but the result in both cases was unfavourable. Appeals were made to the Home Secretary, and all possible political interest brought to bear, but without success. Fauntleroy meanwhile lay in Newgate, not herded with other condemned prisoners, as the custom was, but in a separate chamber, that belonging to one of the warders of the gaol. I find in the chaplain's journal, under date 1824, various entries relative to this prisoner. "Visited Mr. Fauntleroy. My application for books for him not having been granted, I had no prayer-book to give him." "Visited Mr. Fauntleroy. The sheriffs have very kindly permitted him to remain in the turnkey's room where he was originally placed; nor can I omit expressing a hope that this may prove the beginning of a better system of confinement, and that every description of persons who may be unfortunately under sentence of death will no longer be herded indiscriminately together." The kindliness of the city authorities to Fauntleroy was not limited to the assignment of a separate place of durance.

A very curious and, in its way, amusing circumstance in connection with this case was the offer of a certain Italian, Edmund Angelini, to take Fauntleroy's place. Angelini wrote to the Lord Mayor to this effect, urging that Fauntleroy was a father, a citizen: "His life is useful, mine a burthen, to the State." He was summoned to the Mansion House, where he repeated his request, crying, "Accordez moi cette grâce," with much urgency. There were doubts of his sanity. He wrote afterwards to the effect that the moment he had offered himself, an unknown assassin came to aim a blow at him. "Let this monster give his name; I am ready to fight him. I am still determined to put myself in the place of Mr. Fauntleroy. If the law of this country can receive such a sacrifice, my death will render to heaven an innocent man, and to earth a repentant sinner."

The concourse in front of Newgate was enormous at Fauntleroy's execution, but much sympathy was evinced for this unfortunate victim to human weakness and ruthless laws. A report was, moreover, widely circulated, and the impression long prevailed, that he actually escaped death. It was said that strangulation had been prevented by the insertion of a silver tube in his windpipe, and that after hanging for the regulated time he was taken down and easily restored to consciousness. Afterwards, according to the common rumour, he went abroad and lived there for many years; but the story is not only wholly unsubstantiated, but there is good evidence to show that the body after execution was handed over to his friends and interred privately.

Some years were still to elapse before capital punishment ceased to be the penalty for forgery, and in the interval several persons were sentenced and suffered death for this crime. There were two notable capital convictions for forgery in 1828. One was that of Captain Montgomery, who assumed the aliases of Colonel Wallace and Colonel Morgan. His offence was uttering forged notes, and there was strong suspicion that he had long subsisted entirely by this fraud. The act for which he was taken into custody was the payment of a forged ten-pound note for half-a-dozen silver spoons. Montgomery was an adept at forgery. He had gone wrong early. Although born of respectable parents, and gazetted to a commission in the army, he soon left the service and betook himself to dishonest ways. His first forgery was the marvellous imitation of the signature of the Hon. Mr. Neville, M. P., who wrote an extremely cramped and curious hand. He was not prosecuted for this fraud on account of the respectability of his family, and soon after this escape he came to London, where he practised as a professional swindler and cheat. For a long time justice did not overtake him for any criminal offence, but he was frequently in Newgate and in the King's Bench for debt. After three years' confinement in the latter prison he passed himself off as his brother, Colonel Montgomery, a distinguished officer, and would have married an heiress had not the imposture been discovered in time. He then took to forging bank-notes, and was arrested as I have described above. Montgomery was duly sentenced to death, but he preferred suicide to the gallows. After sentence his demeanour was serious yet firm. The night previous to that fixed for his execution he wrote several letters, one of them being to Edward Gibbon Wakefield, a fellow-prisoner, and listened attentively to the ordinary, who read him the well-known address written and delivered by Dr. Dodd previous to his own execution for forgery. But next morning he was found dead in his cell. In one corner after much search a phial was found labelled "Prussic acid," which it was asserted he had been in the habit of carrying about his person ever since he had taken to passing forged notes, as an "antidote against disgrace." This phial he had managed to retain in his possession in spite of the frequent searches to which he was subjected in Newgate.

The second conviction for forgery in 1828 was that of the Quaker Joseph Hunton, a man previously of the highest repute in the city of London. He had prospered in early life, was a slop-seller on a large scale at Bury St. Edmunds, and a sugar-baker in the metropolis. He married a lady also belonging to the Society of Friends, who brought him a large fortune, which, together with his own money, he put into a city firm, that of Dickson and Company. Soon after he became deeply involved in Stock Exchange speculations, and losing heavily, to meet the claims upon him he put out a number of forged bills of exchange or acceptances, to which the signature of one Wilkins of Abingdon was found to be forged. Hunton tried to fly the country on the detection of the fraud, but was arrested at Plymouth just as he was on the point of leaving England in the New York packet. He had gone on board in his Quaker dress, but when captured was found in a light-green frock, a pair of light-gray pantaloons, a black stock and a foraging cap. Hunton was put upon his trial at the Old Bailey, and in due course sentenced to death. His defence was that the forged acceptances would have been met on coming to maturity, and that he had no real desire to defraud. Hunton accepted his sentence with great resignation, although he protested against the inhumanity of the laws which condemned him to death. On entering Newgate he said, "I wish after this day to have communication with nobody; let me take leave of my wife, and family, and friends. I have already suffered an execution; my heart has undergone that horrible penalty." He was, however, visited by and received his wife, and several members of the Society of Friends. Two elders of the meeting sat up with him in the press-yard the whole of the night previous to execution, and a third, Mr. Sparks Moline, came to attend him to the scaffold. He met his death with unshaken firmness, only entreating that a certain blue handkerchief, to which he seemed fondly attached, should be used to bandage his eyes, which request was readily granted.

Hunton's execution no doubt aroused public attention to the cruelty and futility of the capital law against forgery. A society which had already been started against capital punishment devoted its efforts first to a mitigation of the forgery statute, but could not immediately accomplish much. In 1829 the gallows claimed two more victims for this offence. One was Richard Gifford, a well-educated youth who had been at Christ's Hospital, and afterwards in the National Debt Office. Unfortunately he took to drink, lost his appointment, and fell from bad to worse. Suddenly, after reaching the lowest depths, he emerged, and was found by his friends living in comfort in the Waterloo Road. His funds, which he pretended came to him with a rich wife, were really the proceeds of frauds upon the Bank of England. He forged the names of people who held stock on the Bank books, and got the value of the stock; he also forged dividend receipts and got the dividends. He was only six-and-twenty when he was hanged. The other and the last criminal executed for forgery in England was one Maynard, who was convicted of a fraud upon the Custom House. In conjunction with two others, one of whom was a clerk in the Custom House, and had access to the official records, he forged a warrant for £1,973, and was paid the money by the comptroller general. Maynard was convicted of uttering the forged document, Jones of being an accessory; the third prisoner was acquitted. Maynard was the only one who suffered death.

This execution was on the last day of the year 1829. In the following session Sir Robert Peel brought in a bill to consolidate the acts relating to forgery. Upon the third reading of this bill Sir James Macintosh moved as an amendment that capital punishment should be abolished for all crimes of forgery, except the forgery of wills and powers of attorney. This amendment was strongly supported outside the House, and a petition in favour of its passing was presented, signed by more than a thousand members of banking firms. Macintosh's amendment was carried in the Commons, but the new law did not pass the Lords, who re-enacted the capital penalty. Still no sentence of death was carried out for the offence, and in 1832 the Attorney-General introduced a bill to entirely abolish capital punishment for forgery. It passed the Commons, but opposition was again encountered in the Lords. This time they sent the bill back, re-enacting only the two penalties for will forging and the forging of powers of attorney; in other words, they had advanced in 1832 to the point at which the Lower House had arrived in 1830. There were at the moment in Newgate six convicts sentenced to death for forging wills. The question was whether the Government would dare to take their lives at the bidding of the House of Lords, and in defiance of the vote of the assembly which more accurately represented public opinion. It was indeed announced that their fate was sealed; but Mr. Joseph Hume pressed the Government hard, and obtained an assurance that the men should not be executed. The new Forgery Act with the Lords' amendment passed into law, but the latter proved perfectly harmless, and no person ever after suffered death for any variety of this crime.

One of the last instances of a crime which in time past had invariably been visited with the death penalty,[217:1] and which was of a distinctly fraudulent nature should be noted here. The abduction of Miss Turner by the brothers Wakefield bore a strong resemblance to the carrying off and forcible marrying of heiresses as already described in a previous chapter. Miss Turner was a school-girl of barely fifteen, only child of a gentleman of large property in Cheshire, of which county he was actually high sheriff at the time of his daughter's abduction. The elder brother, Edward Gibbon Wakefield, the prime mover in the abduction, was a barrister not exactly briefless, but without a large practice. He had, it was said, a good private income, and was already a widower with two children at the time he committed the offence for which he was subsequently tried. He had eloped with his first wife from school. While on a visit to Macclesfield he heard by chance of Miss Turner, and that she would inherit all her father's possessions. He thereupon conceived an idea of carrying her off and marrying her willy nilly at Gretna Green. The two brothers started at once for Liverpool, where Miss Turner was at school with a Mrs. Daulby. At Manchester, *en route*, a travelling carriage was purchased, which was driven up to Mrs. Daulby's door at eight in the morning, and a servant hurriedly alighted from it, bearing a letter for Miss

Turner. This purported to be from the medical attendant of Mr. Turner, written at Shrigley, Mr. Turner's place of residence; and it stated that Mrs. Turner had been stricken with paralysis. She was not in immediate danger, but she wished to see her daughter, "as it was possible she might soon become incapable of recognizing any one." Miss Turner, greatly agitated, accompanied the messenger who had brought this news, a disguised servant of Wakefield's, who had plausibly explained that he had only recently been engaged at Shrigley. The road taken was viâ Manchester, where the servant said a Dr. Hull was to be picked up to go on with them to Shrigley.

At Manchester, however, the carriage stopped at the Albion Hotel. Miss Turner was shown into a private room, where Mr. Wakefield soon presented himself. Miss Turner, not knowing him, would have left the room, but he said he came from her father, and she remained. Wakefield, in reply to her inquiries, satisfied her that her mother was well, and that the real reason for summoning her from school was the state of her father's affairs. Mr. Turner was on the verge of bankruptcy. He was at that moment at Kendal, and wished her to join him there at once. Miss Turner consented to go on, and they travelled night and day towards the north. But at Kendal there was no Mr. Turner, and, to allay Miss Turner's growing anxiety, Wakefield found it necessary to become more explicit regarding her father's affairs. He now pretended that Mr. Turner was also on his way to the border, pursued by sheriffs' officers. The fact was, Wakefield went on to say, an uncle of his had advanced Mr. Turner £60,000, which had temporarily staved off ruin. But another bank had since failed, and nothing could save Mr. Turner but the transfer of some property to Miss Turner, and its settlement on her, so that it might become the exclusive property of her husband, "whoever he might be." Wakefield added that it had been suggested he should marry Miss Turner, but that he had laughed at the idea. Wakefield's uncle took the matter more seriously, and declared that unless the marriage came off Mr. Turner must be sold up. Miss Turner, thus pressed, consented to go on to Gretna Green. Passing through Carlisle, she was told that Mr. Turner was in the town, but could not show himself. Nothing could release him from his trouble but the arrival of the marriage certificate from Gretna Green. Filial affection rose superior to all scruples, and Miss Turner, having crossed the border, was married to Wakefield by the blacksmith in the usual way. Returning to Carlisle, she now heard that her father had been set free, and had gone home to Shrigley, whither they were to follow him. They set out, but at Leeds Wakefield found himself called suddenly to Paris; the other brother was accordingly sent on a pretended mission to Shrigley to bring Mr. Turner on to London, whither Wakefield and Miss Turner also proceeded. On arrival, Wakefield pretended that they had missed Mr. Turner, and must follow him over to France. The strangely-married couple thereupon pressed on to Dover, and crossed over to Calais.

The fact of the abduction did not transpire for some days. Then Mrs. Daulby learned that Miss Turner had not arrived at Shrigley, but that she had gone to Manchester. Friends went in pursuit and traced her to Huddersfield and further north. The terror and dismay of her parents were soon intensified by the receipt of a letter from Wakefield, at Carlisle, announcing the marriage. Mr. Turner at once set off for London, where he sought the assistance of the police, and presently ascertained that Wakefield had gone to the Continent with his involuntary bride. An uncle of Miss Wakefield's, accompanied by his solicitor and a Bow Street runner, at once went in pursuit. Meanwhile, a second letter turned up from Wakefield at Calais, in which he assured Mrs. Turner that Miss Turner was fondly attached to him, and went on to say, "I do assure you, madam, that it shall be the anxious endeavour of my life to promote her happiness by every means in my power." The game, however, was nearly up. Miss Turner was met by her uncle on Calais pier as she was walking with Wakefield. The uncle claimed her. The husband resisted. M. le Maire was appealed to, and decided to leave it to the young lady, who at once abandoned Wakefield. As he still urged his rights over his wife, Miss Turner cried out in protest, "No, no, I am not his wife; he carried me away by fraud and stratagem, and forced me to accompany him to Gretna Green. . . . By the same forcible means I was compelled to quit England, and to trust myself to the protection of this person, whom I never saw until I was taken from Liverpool, and never want to see again." On this Wakefield gave in. He surrendered the bride who had never been a wife, and she returned to England with her friends, while Wakefield went on alone to Paris.

Mr. William Wakefield was arrested at Dover, conveyed to Chester, and committed to Lancaster Gaol for trial at the next assizes, when indictments were preferred against both brothers "for having carried away Ellen Turner, spinster, then a maid and heir apparent unto her father, for the sake of the lucre of her substance; and for having afterwards unlawfully and against her will married the said Ellen Turner." They were tried in March of the following year, Edward Wakefield having apparently given himself up, and found guilty, remaining in Lancaster Gaol for a couple of months, when they were brought up to the court of King's Bench for judgment. The prosecution pressed for a severe penalty. Edward Wakefield pleaded that his trial had already cost him £3,000. Mr. Justice Bayley, in summing up, spoke severely of the gross deception practised upon an innocent girl, and sentenced the brothers each to three years' imprisonment, William Wakefield in Lancaster Gaol, and Edward Gibbon Wakefield in Newgate, which sentences were duly enforced. The marriage was annulled by an Act of Parliament, although Wakefield petitioned against it, and was brought from Newgate, at his own request, to oppose the second reading of the bill. He also wrote and published a pamphlet from the gaol to show that Miss Turner had been a consenting party to the marriage, and was really his wife. Neither his address nor his pamphlet availed much, for the bill for the divorce passed both Houses.

Having brought down the record of great frauds and forgeries to the third and fourth decades of the nineteenth century some account must be given of the more remarkable murders during that period.

No murder has created greater sensation and horror throughout England than that of Mr. Weare by Thurtell, Hunt and Probert. The principal actor was tried and executed at Hertford, but Probert, who turned King's evidence and materially assisted conviction, was tried at the Old Bailey the following year for horse-stealing, and hanged in front of Newgate. The murder was still fresh in the memory of the populace, and Probert was all but lynched on his way to gaol. According to his statement, when sentenced to death, he had been driven to horse-stealing by the execration which had pursued him after the murder. Every door had been closed against him, every hope of future support blasted. "Since the calamitous event that happened at Hertford, I have been a lost man." The event which he styles calamitous we may well characterize as one of the most deliberately atrocious murders on record. Thurtell was a gambler, and Weare had won a good deal of money from him. Weare was supposed to carry a "private bank" about with him in a pocket in his under waistcoat. To obtain possession of this, Thurtell with his two associates resolved to kill him. The victim was invited to visit Probert's cottage in the country near Elstree. Thurtell drove him down in a gig, "to be killed as he travelled," in Thurtell's own words. The others followed, and on overtaking Thurtell, found he had done the job alone in a retired part of the road known as Gill's Hill Lane. The murderer explained that he had first fired a pistol at Weare's head, but the shot glanced off his cheek. Then he attacked the other's throat with a penknife, and last of all drove the pistol barrel into his forehead. After the murder the villains divided the spoil, and went on to Probert's cottage, and supped off pork-chops brought down on purpose. During the night they sought to dispose of the body by throwing it into a pond, but two days later had to throw it into another pond. Meanwhile the discovery of pistol and knife spattered with human blood and brains raised the alarm, and suspicion fell upon the three murderers, who were arrested. The crime was brought home to Thurtell by the confession of Hunt, one of his accomplices, who took the police to the pond, where the remains of the unfortunate Mr. Weare were discovered, sunk in a sack weighted by stones. Probert was then admitted as a witness, and the case was fully proved against Thurtell, who was hanged in front of Hertford Gaol. Hunt, in consideration of the information he had given, escaped death, and was sentenced to transportation for life.

Widespread horror and indignation was evoked throughout the kingdom by the discovery of the series of atrocious murders perpetrated in Edinburgh by the miscreants Burke and Hare, the first of whom has added to the British language a synonym for illegal suppression. The crimes of these inhuman purveyors to medical science do not fall within the limits of this work. But Burke and Hare had their imitators further south, and of these Bishop and Williams, who were guilty of many peculiar atrocities, ended their murderous careers in front of the debtors' door at Newgate. Bishop, whose real name was Head, married a half-sister of Williams'. Williams was a professional resurrectionist, or body-snatcher, a trade almost openly countenanced when "subjects" for the anatomy schools were only to be got by rifling graves, or worse. Bishop was a carpenter, but having been suddenly thrown out of work, he joined his brother-in-law in his line of business. After a little Bishop got weary of the dangers and fatigues of exhumation, and proposed to Williams that instead of disinterring they should murder their subjects. Bishop confessed that he was moved to this by the example of Burke and Hare. They pursued their terrible trade for five years without scruple and without detection. Eventually the law overtook them, but almost by accident. They presented themselves about noon one day at the dissecting room of King's College Hospital, accompanied by a third man, an avowed "snatcher" and *habitué* of the "Fortune of War," a public-house in Smithfield frequented openly by men of this awful profession. This man, May, asked the porter at King's College if "he wanted anything?" the euphemism for offering a body. The porter asked what he had got, and the answer was, a male subject. Reference was made to Mr. Partridge, the demonstrator in anatomy, and after some haggling they agreed on a price, and in the afternoon the snatchers brought a hamper which contained a body in a sack. The porter received it, but from its freshness became suspicious of foul play. Mr. Partridge was sent for, and he with some of the students soon decided that the corpse had not died a natural death. The snatchers were detained, the police sent for, and arrest followed as a matter of course.

An inquest was held on the body, which was identified as that of an Italian boy, Carlo Ferrari, who made a living by exhibiting white mice about the streets, and the jury returned a verdict of wilful murder against persons unknown, expressing a strong opinion that Bishop, Williams, and May had been concerned in the transaction. Meanwhile, a search had been made at Nova Scotia Gardens, Bethnal Green, where Bishop and Williams lived. At first nothing peculiar was found; but at a second search the back-garden ground was dug up, and in one corner, at some depth, a bundle of clothes were unearthed, which, with a hairy cap, were known to be what Ferrari had worn when last seen. In another portion of the garden more clothing, partly male and partly female, was discovered, plainly pointing to the perpetration of other crimes. These facts were represented before the police magistrate who examined Bishop and his fellows, and further incriminating evidence adduced, to the effect that the prisoners had bartered for a coach to carry "a stiff 'un;" they had also been seen to leave their cottage, carrying out a sack with something heavy inside. On this they were fully committed to Newgate for trial. This trial came off in due course at the Central Criminal Court, where the prisoners were charged on two counts, one that of the murder of the Italian boy, the other that of a boy unknown. The evidence from first to last was circumstantial, but the jury, after a short deliberation, did not hesitate to bring in a verdict of guilty, and all three were condemned to death.

Shortly before the day fixed for execution, Bishop made a full confession, the bulk of which bore the impress of truth, although it included statements that were improbable and unsubstantiated. He asserted that the victim was a Lincolnshire lad, and not an Italian boy, although the latter was fully proved. According to the confession, death had been inflicted by drowning in a well, whereas the medical evidence all pointed to violence. It was, however, pretty clear that this victim, like preceding ones, had been lured to Nova Scotia Gardens, and there drugged with a large dose of laudanum. While they were in a state of insensibility the murder was committed. Bishop's confession was endorsed by Williams, and the immediate result was the respite of May. A very painful scene occurred in Newgate when the news of his escape from death was imparted to May. He fainted, and the warrant of mercy nearly proved his death-blow. The other two looked on at his agitation with an indifference amounting to apathy. The execution took place a week or two later, in the presence of such a crowd as had not been seen near Newgate for years.

The murder of Hannah Brown is still fresh in the minds of Londoners, although half a century has passed since it was committed. The horror with which Greenacre's crime struck the town was unparalleled since the time when Catherine Hayes slew her husband. There were many features of resemblance in these crimes. The decapitation and dismemberment, the bestowal of the remains in various parts of the town, the preservation of the head in spirits of wine, in the hope that the features might some day be recognized, were alike in both. The murder in both cases was long a profound mystery. In this which I am now describing, a bricklayer found a human trunk near some new buildings in the Edgeware Road one morning in the last week of 1836. The inquest on these remains, which medical examination showed to be those of a female, returned a verdict of wilful murder against some person unknown. Early in January, 1837, the lockman of "Ben Jonson lock," in Stepney Fields, found a human head jammed into the lock gates. Closer investigation proved that it belonged to the trunk already discovered as mentioned above. A further discovery was made in an osier bed near Cold Harbour Lane, Camberwell, where a workman found a bundle containing two human legs, in a drain. These were the missing members of the same mutilated trunk, and there was now evidence sufficient to establish conclusively that the woman thus collected piecemeal had been barbarously done to death. But the affair still remained a profound mystery. No light was thrown upon it till, towards the end of March, a Mr. Gay of Goodge Street came to view the head, and immediately recognized it as that of a widowed sister, Hannah Brown, who had been missing since the previous Christmas Day.

The murdered individual was thus identified. The next step was to ascertain where and with whom she had last been seen. This brought suspicion on to a certain James Greenacre, whom she was to have married, and in whose company she had left her own lodgings to visit his in Camberwell. The police wished to refer to Greenacre, but as he was not forthcoming, a warrant was issued for his apprehension, which was effected at Kennington on the 24th March. A woman named Gale, who lived with him, was arrested at the same time. The prisoners were examined at the Marylebone police court. Greenacre, a stout, middle-aged man, wrapped in a brown greatcoat, assumed an air of insolent bravado; but his despair must have been great, as was evident from his attempt to strangle himself in the station-house. Suspicion grew almost to a certainty as the evidence was unfolded. Mrs. Brown was a washerwoman, supposed to be worth some money; hence Greenacre's offer of marriage. She had realized all her effects, and brought them with her furniture to Greenacre's lodgings. The two when married were to emigrate to Hudson's Bay. Whether it was greed or a quarrel that drove Greenacre to the desperate deed remains obscure. They were apparently good friends when last seen together at a neighbour's, where they seemed "perfectly happy and sociable, and eager for the wedding day." But Greenacre in his confession pretended that he and his intended had quarrelled over her property or the want of it, and that in a moment of anger he knocked her down. He thought he had killed her, and in his terror began at once to consider how he might dispose of the body and escape arrest. While she was senseless, but really still alive, he cut off her head, and dismembered the body in the manner already described. It is scarcely probable that he would have gone to this extremity if he had had no previous evil intention, and the most probable inference is that he inveigled Mrs. Brown to his lodgings with the set purpose of taking her life.

His measures for the disposal of the *corpus delicti* remind us of those taken by Mrs. Hayes and her associates, or of Gardelle's frantic efforts to conceal his crime. The most ghastly part of the story is that which deals with his disposal of the head. This, wrapped up in a silk handkerchief, he carried under his coat-flaps through the streets, and afterwards on his cap in a crowded city omnibus. It was not until he left the 'bus, and walked up by the Regent's Canal, that he conceived the idea of throwing the head into the water. Another day elapsed before he got rid of the rest of the body, all of which, according to his own confession, made with the idea of exonerating Mrs. Gale, he accomplished without her assistance. On the other hand, it was adduced in evidence that Mrs. Gale had been at his lodgings the very day after the murder, and was seen to be busily engaged in washing down the house with bucket and mop.

Greenacre, when tried at the Old Bailey, admitted that he had been guilty of manslaughter. While conversing with Mrs. Brown, he declared the unfortunate woman was rocking herself to and fro in a chair; as she leaned back he put his foot against the chair, and so tilted it over. Mrs. Brown fell with it, and Greenacre, to his horror, found that she was dead. But the medical evidence was clear that the decapitation had been effected during life, and the jury, after a short deliberation, without hesitation brought in a verdict of wilful murder. The woman Gale was also found guilty, but sentence of death was passed only on Greenacre. The execution was, as usual, attended by an immense concourse, and Greenacre died amidst the loudest execrations. Gale was sentenced to penal servitude for life.

The gravest crimes continued at intervals to inspire the town with horror, and concentrate public attention upon the gaol of Newgate, and the murderers immured within its walls. Courvoisier's case made a great stir. There was unusual atrocity in this murder of an aged, infirm gentleman, a scion of the ducal house of Bedford, by his confidential valet and personal attendant. Lord William Russell lived alone in Norfolk Street, Park Lane. He was a widower, and seventy-three years of age. One morning in May his lordship was found dead in his bed with his throat cut. The fact of the murder was first discovered by the housemaid, who, on going down early, was surprised to find the dining-room in a state of utter confusion; the furniture turned upside down, the drawers of the escritoire open and rifled, a bundle lying on the floor, as though thieves had been interrupted in the act. The housemaid summoned the cook, and both went to call the valet, Courvoisier, who came from his room ready dressed, a suspicious circumstance, as he was always late in the morning. The housemaid suggested that they should see if his lordship was all right, and the three went to his bed-room. While Courvoisier opened the shutters, the housemaid, approaching the bed, saw that the pillow was saturated with blood.

The discovery of the murdered man immediately followed. The neighbourhood was alarmed, the police sent for, and a close inquiry forthwith commenced. That Lord William Russell had committed suicide was at once declared impossible. It was also clearly proved that no forcible entry had been made into the house; the fresh marks of violence upon the door had evidently been made inside, and not from outside; moreover, the instruments, poker and chisel, by which they had no doubt been effected, were found in the butler's pantry, used by Courvoisier. The researches of the police soon laid bare other suspicious facts. The bundle found in the dining-room contained, with clothes, various small articles of plate and jewelry which a thief would probably have put into his pocket. Upstairs in the bed-room a *rouleaux* box for sovereigns had been broken open, also the jewel-box and note-case, from the latter of which was abstracted a ten-pound note known to have been in the possession of the deceased. His lordship's watch was gone. Further suspicion was caused by the position of a book and a wax candle by the bedside. The latter was so placed that it would throw no light on the book, which was a "Life of Sir Samuel Romilly." The intention of the real murderer to shift the crime to burglars was evident although futile, and the police, feeling convinced that the crime had been committed by some inmate of the house, took Courvoisier into custody, and placed the two female servants under surveillance. The valet's strange demeanour had attracted attention from the first. He had hung over the body in a state of dreadful agitation, answering no questions, and taking no part in the proceedings.

Three days later a close search of the butler's pantry produced fresh circumstantial evidence. Behind the skirting board several of his lordship's rings were discovered; near it was his Waterloo medal, and the above-mentioned ten-pound note. Further investigation was rewarded by the discovery in the pantry of a split gold ring, used by Lord William, to carry his keys on; next, and in the same place, a chased gold key; and at last his lordship's watch was found secreted under the leads of the sink. All this was evidence sufficient to warrant Courvoisier's committal for trial; but still he found friends, and a liberal subscription was raised among the foreign servants in London to provide funds for his defence. Courvoisier, when put on his trial, pleaded not guilty; but on the second day the discovery of fresh evidence, more particularly the recovery of some of Lord William's stolen plate, induced the prisoner to make a full confession of his crime to the lawyers who defended him. This placed them in a position of much embarrassment. To have thrown up their brief would have been to have secured Courvoisier's conviction. Mr. Phillips, who led in the case, went to the other extreme, and in an impassioned address implored the jury not to send an innocent man to the gallows. It will be remembered that the question whether Mr. Phillips had not exceeded the limits usually allowed to counsel was much debated at the time.

The jury without hesitation found Courvoisier guilty, and he was sentenced to death. The prisoner's demeanour had greatly changed during the trial. Coolness amounting almost to effrontery gave way to hopeless dejection. On his removal to Newgate after sentence, he admitted that he had been justly convicted, and expressed great anxiety that his fellow-servants should be relieved from all suspicion. Later in the day he tried to commit suicide by cramming a towel down his throat, but was prevented. Next morning he made a full confession in presence of his attorney, and the governor, Mr. Cope. In this he gave as the motives of his crime a quarrel he had with his master, who threatened to discharge him without a character. Lord William, according to the valet, was of a peevish, difficult temper; he was annoyed with his man for various small omissions and acts of forgetfulness, and on the night of the murder had taken Courvoisier to task rather sharply. Finally, on coming downstairs after bed-time, Lord William had found Courvoisier in the dining-room. "What are you doing here?" asked his lordship. "You can have no good intentions; you must quit my service to-morrow morning." This seems to have decided Courvoisier, who took a carving-knife from the side-board in the dining-room, went upstairs to Lord William's bed-room, and drew the knife across his throat. "He appeared to die instantly," said the murderer, in conclusion. His account of his acts and movements after the deed varied so considerably in the several documents he left behind, that too much reliance cannot be placed upon his confession. His last statement contains the words, "The public now think I am a liar, and they will not believe me when I say the truth." This was no doubt the case, but this much truth his confession may be taken to contain: that Courvoisier was idle, discontented, ready to take offence, greedy of gain; that he could not resist the opportunity of robbery offered him by his situation at Lord William Russell's; that when vexed with his master he did not shrink from murder, both for revenge and to conceal his other crimes.

Courvoisier wished to commit suicide in Newgate, but was prevented by the vigilant supervision to which he was subjected while in gaol. The attempt was to have been made by opening a vein and allowing himself to bleed to death. The Sunday night before his execution he would not go to bed when ordered. The governor insisted, but Courvoisier showed great reluctance to strip. The order was, however, at length obeyed, and the whole of the prisoner's clothes were minutely searched. In the pocket of the coat Mr. Cope, the governor, found a neatly folded cloth, and asked what it was for. Courvoisier admitted that he had intended to bind it tightly round his arm and bleed himself to death in the night. The next inquiry was how he hoped to open a vein. "With a bit of sharpened stick picked out of the ordinary firewood." "Where is it?" asked the governor. The prisoner replied that he had left it in the mattress of which he had just been deprived. The bed was searched, but no piece of sharpened wood was found. It was thought that it might have been lost in changing the mattresses. The cloth above referred to belonged to the inner seam of his trousers, which he had managed to tear out. There is nothing to show that Courvoisier really contemplated self-destruction.

A murder which reproduced many of the features of that committed by Greenacre soon followed, and excited the public mind even more than that of Courvoisier's. Daniel Good's crime might have remained long undiscovered but for his own careless stupidity. He was coachman to a gentleman at Roehampton. One day he went into a pawnbroker's at Wandsworth, and bought a pair of breeches on credit. At the same time he was seen to steal and secrete a pair of trousers. The shop-boy gave information. Good was followed to his stables by a policeman, but obstinately denied the theft. The policeman insisted on searching the premises, at which Good displayed some uneasiness. This increased when the officer, accompanied by two others, a neighbour and a bailiff, entered one of the stables. Good now offered to go to Wandsworth and satisfy the pawnbroker. Just at this moment, however, the searchers found concealed under two trusses of hay a woman's headless and dismembered trunk. At the constable's cry of alarm Good rushed from the stable and locked the door behind him. Some time elapsed before the imprisoned party could force open the doors, and by then the fugitive had escaped. Medical assistance having been summoned, it was ascertained how the dismemberment had been effected. At the same time an overpowering odour attracted them to the adjoining harness-room, where the missing remains were raked out half consumed in the ashes of a wood fire. In the same room a large axe and saw were found covered with blood.

Inquiry into the character of Good exposed him as a loose liver, who "kept company" with several women. One called his sister, but supposed to be his wife, had occupied a room in South Street, Manchester Square, with a son of Good's by a former wife. Another wife, real or fictitious, existed in Spitalfields, and evidence was given of close relation between Good and a third woman, a girl named Butcher, residing at Woolwich. The victim was the first of these three. Good had told her, much to her perturbation, that she was to move from South Street to Roehampton, and one day he fetched her. They were seen together on Barnes Common, and again in Putney Park Lane, where they were talking loud and angrily. The poor creature was never seen again alive. The actual method of the murder was never exactly ascertained. Good himself remained at large for some weeks. He had tramped as far as Tunbridge, where he obtained work as a bricklayer's labourer; he there gave satisfaction for industry, but he was taciturn, and would hold no converse with his fellows. The woman where he lodged noticed that he was very restless at night, moaning and sighing much. Detection came unexpectedly. He was recognized by an ex-policeman who had known him at Roehampton, and immediately arrested. In his effects were found the clothes he had on at the time of his escape from the stables, and under the jacket he was wearing was a piece of a woman's calico apron stained with blood, which he had used to save the pressure on his shoulder by the hod. Good was committed to Newgate, and tried at the Central Criminal Court before a crowded court. He made a rambling defence, ending by saying, "Good ladies and gentlemen all, I have a great deal more to say, but I am so bad I cannot say it." The case was clearly proved against him, and he was condemned, sentenced, and duly executed.

Hocker's murder is in its way interesting, as affording another proof of the extraordinary way in which the culprit returned to the scene of his guilt. The cries of his victim, a Mr. Delarue, brought passers-by and policemen to the spot, a lonely place near a dead wall beyond Belsize Hall, Hampstead, but too late to give substantial aid. While the body lay there still warm, battered and bleeding from the cruel blows inflicted upon him by his cowardly assailant, a man came by singing. He entered into conversation with the policemen, and learned, as it seemed for the first time, what had happened. His remark was, "It is a nasty job;" he took hold of the dead hand, and confessed that he felt "queer" at the shocking sight. This sight was his own handiwork, yet he could not overcome the strange fascination it had for him, and remained by the side of the corpse till the stretcher came. Even then he followed it as far as Belsize Lane. It was here that the others engaged in their dismal office of removing the dead first got a good look at the stranger's face. He wanted a light for a cigar, and got it from a lantern which was lifted up and fully betrayed his features. It was noticed that he wore a mackintosh. Next day the police, in making a careful search of the scene of the murder, picked up a coat-button, which afterwards played an important part in the identification of the murderer. A letter, which afforded an additional clue, was also found in the pocket of the deceased. Still it was many weeks before any arrest was made. In the meantime the police were not idle. It came out by degrees that the person who had been seen in Belsize Lane on the night the body was found was a friend of the deceased. His name was Hocker; he was by trade a ladies' shoemaker; and it was also ascertained that after the day of the murder he was flush of money. He was soon afterwards arrested on suspicion, and a search of his lodgings brought to light several garments saturated with blood; a coat among them much torn and stained, with three buttons missing, one of which corresponded with that picked up at Hampstead. The letter found in the pocket of the deceased was sealed with a wafer marked F, and many of the same sort were found in the possession of the accused. This was enough to obtain a committal, after several remands; but the case contained elements of doubt, and the evidence at the trial was entirely circumstantial. A witness deposed to meeting Hocker, soon after the cries of murder were heard, running at a dog-trot into London, and others swore that they plainly recognized him as the man seen soon afterwards in the lane. A woman whom he called on the same evening declared he had worn a mackintosh, his coat was much torn, there was a stain of blood on his shirt-cuff, and he was in possession, the first time to her knowledge, of a watch. This was Delarue's watch, fully identified as such, which Hocker told his brother Delarue had given him the morning of the murder.

These were damnatory facts which well supported the prosecution. The prisoner made an elaborate defence, in which he sought to vilify the character of the deceased as the seducer of an innocent girl to whom he (Hocker) had been fondly attached. When her ruin was discovered her brother panted for revenge. Hocker, whose skill in counterfeiting handwriting was known, was asked to fabricate a letter making an assignation with Delarue in a lonely part of Hampstead. Hocker and the brother went to the spot, where the latter left him to meet his sister's seducer alone. Soon afterwards Hocker heard cries of "murder," and proceeding to where they came from, found Delarue dead, slain by the furious brother. Hocker was so overcome, feeling himself the principal cause of the tragedy, that he rushed to a slaughter-house in Hampstead and purposely stained his clothes with blood. Such an extravagant defence did not weigh with judge or jury; the first summed up dead against the prisoner, and the latter, after retiring for ten minutes, found him guilty. Hocker's conduct in Newgate while under sentence of death was most extraordinary. He drew up several long statements, containing narratives purely fictitious, imputing crimes to his victim, and repeating his line of defence, that Delarue had suffered by the hands of imaginary outraged brothers acting as the avengers of females deeply injured by him. Hocker made several pretended confessions and revelations, all of which were proved to be absolutely false by the police on inquiry. His demeanour was a strange compound of wickedness, falsehood, and deceit. But at the fatal hour his hardihood forsook him, and he was almost insensible when taken out of his cell for execution. Restoratives were applied, but he was in a fainting condition when tied, and had to be supported by the assistant executioner while Calcraft adjusted the noose.

There was an epidemic of murder in the United Kingdom about 1848-9. In November of the first-named year occurred the wholesale slaughter of the Jermys in their house, Stanfield Hall, by the miscreant Rush. Soon afterwards, in Gloucestershire, a maidservant, Sarah Thomas, murdered her mistress, an aged woman, by beating out her brains with a stone. Next year John Gleeson Wilson, at Liverpool, murdered a woman, Ann Henrichson, also a maidservant and two children; while in Ireland a wife dashed out her husband's brains with a hammer. London did not escape the contagion, and prominent among the detestable crimes of the period stands that of the Mannings at Bermondsey. These great criminals suffered at Horsemonger Lane Gaol, but they were tried at the Central Criminal Court, and were for some time inmates of Newgate. Their victim was a man named Patrick O'Connor, a Custom-House gauger, who had been a suitor of Marie de Roux before she became Mrs. Manning. Marie de Roux up to the time of her marriage had been in service as lady's-maid to Lady Blantyre, daughter of the Duchess of Sutherland, and Manning hoped to get some small Government appointment through his wife's interest. He had failed in this as well as in the business of a publican, which he had at one time adopted. After the marriage a close intimacy was still maintained between O'Connor and the Mannings. He lived at Mile End, whence he walked often to call at No. 3, Minver Place, Bermondsey, the residence of his old love. O'Connor was a man of substance. He had long followed the profitable trade of a money-lender, and by dint of usurious interest on small sums advanced to needy neighbours, had amassed as much as ten thousand pounds. His wealth was well known to "Maria," as he called Mrs. Manning, who made several ineffectual attempts to get money out of him. At last this fiendish woman made up her mind to murder O'Connor and appropriate all his possessions. Her husband, to whom she coolly confided her intention, a heavy brutish fellow, was yet aghast at his wife's resolve, and tried hard to dissuade her from her bad purpose. In his confession after sentence he declared that she plied him well with brandy at this period, and that during the whole time he was never in his right senses. Meanwhile this woman, unflinching in her cold, bloody determination, carefully laid all her plans for the consummation of the deed.

One fine afternoon in August, O'Connor was met walking in the direction of Bermondsey. He was dressed with particular care, as he was to dine at the Mannings, and meet friends, one a young lady. He was seen afterwards smoking and talking with his hosts in their back parlour, and never seen again alive. It came out in the husband's confession that Mrs. Manning induced O'Connor to go down to the kitchen to wash his hands, that she followed him to the basement, that she stood behind him as he stood near the open grave she herself had dug for him, and which he mistook for a drain, and that while he was speaking to her she put the muzzle of the pistol close to the back of his head and shot him down. She ran upstairs, told her husband, made him go down and look at her handiwork, and as O'Connor was not quite dead, Manning gave the *coup de grâce* with a crowbar. After this Mrs. Manning changed her dress and went off in a cab to O'Connor's lodgings, which, having possessed herself of the murdered man's keys, she rifled from end to end. Returning to her own home, where Manning meantime had been calmly smoking and talking to the neighbours over the basement wall, the corpse lying just inside the kitchen all the while, the two set to work to strip the body and hide it under the stones of the floor. This job was not completed till the following day, as the hole had to be enlarged, and the only tool they had was a dust-shovel. A quantity of quicklime was thrown in with the body to destroy all identification. This was on a Thursday evening. For the remainder of that week and part of the next the murderers stayed in the house, and occupied the kitchen, close to the remains of their victim. On the Sunday Mrs. Manning roasted a goose at this same kitchen fire, and ate it with relish in the afternoon. This cold-blooded indifference after the event was only outdone by the premeditation of this horrible murder. The hole must have been excavated and the quicklime purchased quite three weeks before O'Connor met his death, and during that time he must frequently have stood or sat over his own grave.

Discovery of the murder came in this wise. O'Connor, a punctual and well-conducted official, was at once missed at the London Docks. On the third day his friends began to inquire for him, and at their request two police officers were sent to Bermondsey to inquire for him at the Mannings, with whom it was well known that he was very intimate. The Mannings had seen or heard nothing of him, of course. As O'Connor still did not turn up, the police after a couple of days returned to Minver Place. The house was empty, bare and stripped of all its furniture, and its former occupants had decamped. The circumstance was suspicious, and a search was at once made of the whole premises. In the back kitchen one of the detectives remarked that the cement between certain stones looked lighter than the rest, and on trying it with a knife, he found that it was soft and new, while elsewhere it was set and hard. The stones were at once taken up; beneath them was a layer of fresh mortar, beneath that a lot of loose earth, amongst which a stocking was turned up, and presently a human toe. Six inches lower the body of O'Connor was uncovered. He was lying on his face, his legs tied up to his hips so as to allow of the body fitting into the hole. The lime had done its work so rapidly that the features would have been indistinguishable but for the prominent chin and a set of false teeth.

The corpse settled all doubts, and the next point was to lay hands upon the Mannings. It was soon ascertained that the wife had gone off in a cab with a quantity of luggage. Part of this she had deposited to be left till called for at one station, while she had gone herself to another, that at Euston Square. At the first, the boxes were impounded, opened, and found to contain many of O'Connor's effects. At the second, exact information was obtained of Mrs. Manning's movements. She had gone to Edinburgh. A telegraphic message, then newly adapted to the purposes of criminal detection, advised the Edinburgh police of the whole affair, and within an hour an answer was telegraphed stating that Mrs. Manning was in custody. She had been to brokers to negotiate the sale of certain foreign railway stock, with which they had been warned from London not to deal, and they had given information to the police. Her arrest was planned, and, when the telegram arrived from London, completed. An examination of her boxes disclosed a quantity of O'Connor's property. Mrs. Manning was transferred to London and lodged in the Horsemonger Lane Gaol, where her husband soon afterwards joined her. He had fled to Jersey, where he was recognized and arrested. Each tried to throw the blame on the other; Manning declared his wife had committed the murder, Mrs. Manning indignantly denying the charge.

The prisoners were in due course transferred to Newgate, to be put upon their trial at the Central Criminal Court. A great number of distinguished people assembled as usual at the Old Bailey on the day of trial. The Mannings were arraigned together; the husband standing at one of the front corners of the dock, his wife at the other end. Manning, who was dressed in black, appeared to be a heavy, bull-necked, repulsive-looking man, with a very fair complexion and light hair. Mrs. Manning was not without personal charms; her face was comely, she had dark hair and good eyes, and was above the middle height, yet inclined to be stout. She was smartly dressed in a plaid shawl, a white lace cap; her hair was dressed in long *crêpe* bands. She had lace ruffles at her wrist, and wore primrose-coloured kid gloves. The case rested upon the facts which have been already set forth, and was proved to the satisfaction of the jury, who brought in a verdict of guilty. Manning, when sentence of death was passed on him, said nothing; but Mrs. Manning, speaking in a foreign accent, addressed the court with great fluency and vehemence. She complained that she had no justice; there was no law for her, she had found no protection either from judges, the prosecutor, or her husband. She had not been treated like a Christian, but like a wild beast of the forest. She declared that the money found in her possession had been sent her from abroad; that O'Connor had been more to her than her husband, that she ought to have married him. It was against common sense to charge her with murdering the only friend she had in the world: the culprit was really her husband, who killed O'Connor out of jealousy and revengeful feelings. When the judge assumed the black cap Mrs. Manning became still more violent, shouting, "No, no, I will not stand it! You ought to be ashamed of yourselves!" and would have left the dock had not Mr. Cope, the governor of Newgate, restrained her. After judgment was passed, she repeatedly cried out "Shame!" and stretching out her hand, she gathered up a quantity of the rue which, following ancient custom dating from the days of the gaol fever, was strewn in front of the dock, and sprinkled it towards the bench with a contemptuous gesture.

On being removed to Newgate from the court Mrs. Manning became perfectly furious. She uttered loud imprecations, cursing judge, jury, barristers, witnesses, and all who stood around. Her favourite and most often-repeated expression was, "D—n seize you all." They had to handcuff her by force against the most violent resistance, and still she raged and stormed, shaking her clenched and manacled hands in the officers' faces. From Newgate the Mannings were taken in separate cabs to Horsemonger Lane Gaol. On this journey her manner changed completely. She became flippant, joked with the officers, asked how they liked her "resolution" in the dock, and expressed the utmost contempt for her husband, whom she never intended to acknowledge or speak to again. Later her mood changed to abject despair. On reaching the condemned cell she threw herself upon the floor and shrieked in an hysterical agony of tears. After this, until the day of execution, she recovered her spirits, and displayed reckless effrontery, mocking at the chaplain, and turning a deaf ear to the counsels of a benevolent lady who came to visit. Now she abused the jury, now called Manning a vagabond, and through all ate heartily at every meal, slept soundly at nights, and talked with cheerfulness on almost any subject. Nevertheless, she attempted to commit suicide by driving her nails, purposely left long, into her throat. She was discovered just as she was getting black in the face. Manning's demeanour was more in harmony with his situation, and the full confession he made elucidated all dark and uncertain points in connection with the crime. The actual execution, which took place at another prison than Newgate, is rather beyond the scope of this work. But it may be mentioned that the concourse was so enormous that it drew down the well-merited and trenchant disapproval of Charles Dickens, who wrote to the *Times* in the following words: "A sight so inconceivably awful as the wickedness and levity of the immense crowd collected at the execution this morning could be imagined by no man, and presented by no heathen land under the sun. The horrors of the gibbet, and of the crime which brought the wretched murderers to it, faded in my mind before the atrocious bearing, looks and language of the assembled spectators. When I came upon the scene at midnight, the shrillness of the cries and howls that were raised from time to time, denoting that they came from a concourse of boys and girls already assembled in the best places, made my blood run cold." It will be in the memory of many that Mrs. Manning appeared on the scaffold in a black satin dress, which was bound tightly round her waist. This preference brought the costly stuff into disrepute, and its unpopularity lasted for nearly thirty years.

FOOTNOTES:

[217:1] At Liverpool, in 1842, there was a case of abduction, and the well-known case of Mr. Carden and Miss Arbuthnot in Ireland occurred as late as 1854.

CHAPTER IX
LATER RECORDS

Later records of crimes—First private execution under the new law—
Poisoning, revived and more terrible—Palmer's case—His imitators—
Dove—Dr. Smethurst—Catherine Wilson—Piracy and murder—The
"Flowery Land"—Arrest of the mutineers—Their trial and sentence—
Murder of Mr. Briggs in a railway carriage—Pursuit of murderer and his
arrest in New York—Müller's conviction—Confesses guilt—A forged
pardon—The Muswell Hill murder—Bidwell brothers defraud the Bank of
England of £100,000—Sentenced to penal servitude for life—Pentonville
erected—The best type of prison construction—Gradual reformation in
Newgate—The new prison at Holloway—The end of Newgate.

Executions long continued to be in public, in spite of remonstrance and
reprobation. The old prejudices, such as that which enlisted Dr. Johnson on
the side of the Tyburn procession, still lingered and prevented any change. It
was thought that capital punishment would lose its deterrent effect if it
ceased to be public, and the *raison d'être* of the penalty, which in principle so
many opposed, would be gone. This line of argument prevailed over the
manifest horrors of the spectacle.

Already the urgent necessity for abolishing public executions had been
brought before the House of Commons by Mr. Hibbert, and the question,
as part of the whole subject of capital punishment, had been referred to a
royal commission in January of 1864. Full evidence was taken on all points,
and on that regarding public executions there was a great preponderance of
opinion towards their abolition, yet the witnesses were not unanimous. Some
of the judges would have retained the public spectacle; the ordinary of
Newgate was not certain that public executions were not the best. Another
distinguished witness feared that any secrecy in the treatment of the
condemned would invest them with a new and greater interest, which was
much to be deprecated. Foreign witnesses, too, were in favour of publicity.
On the other hand, Lords Cranworth and Wensleydale recommended private
executions, as did Mr. Spencer Walpole, M. P. Sir George Grey thought there
was a growing feeling in favour of executions within the prison precincts.
Colonel (Sir Edmund) Henderson was strongly in favour of them, based on
his own experience in Western Australia. He not only thought them likely to
be more deterrent, but believed that a public ceremony destroyed the whole
value of an execution. Other officials, great lawyers, governors of prisons,
and chaplains supported this view. The only doubts expressed were as to the
sufficiency of the safeguards, as to the certainty of death and its subsequent

publication. But these, it was thought, might be provided by the admission of the press and the holding of a coroner's inquest.

Duly impressed with the weight of evidence in favour of abolition, the commission recommended that death sentences should be carried out within the gaol, "under such regulations as might be considered necessary to prevent abuses and satisfy the public that the law had been complied with." But it is curious to note that there were several dissentients among the commissioners to this paragraph of the report. The judge of the Admiralty Court, the Right Hon. Stephen Lushington, the Right Hon. James Moncrieff, Lord Advocate, Mr. Charles Neate, Mr. William Ewart, and last, but not least, Mr. John Bright declared that they were not prepared to agree to the resolution respecting private executions. Nevertheless, in the very next session a bill was introduced by Mr. Hibbert, M. P., and accepted by the Government, providing for the future carrying out of executions within prisons. It was read for the first time in March, 1866, but did not become law till 1868.

The last public execution in front of Newgate was that of the Fenian Michael Barrett, who was convicted of complicity in the Clerkenwell explosion, intended to effect the release of Burke and Casey from Clerkenwell prison, by which many persons lost their lives. Unusual precautions were taken upon this occasion, as some fresh outrage was apprehended. There was no interference with the crowd, which collected as usual, although not to the customary extent. But Newgate and its neighbourhood were carefully held by the police, both city and metropolitan. In the houses opposite the prison numbers of detectives mixed with the spectators; inside the gaol was Colonel Frazer, the chief commissioner of the city police, and at no great distance, although in the background, troops were held in readiness to act if required. Everything passed off quietly, however, and Calcraft, who had been threatened with summary retribution if he executed Barrett, carried out the sentence without mishap. The sufferer was stolid and reticent to the last.

The first private execution under the new law took place within the precincts of Maidstone Gaol. The sufferer was a porter on the London, Chatham, and Dover railway, sentenced to death for shooting the station-master at Dover. The ceremony, which was witnessed by only a few officials and representatives of the press, was performed with the utmost decency and decorum. The fact that the execution was to take place within the privacy of the gloomy walls, a fact duly advertised as completed by the hoisting of the black flag over the gaol, had undoubtedly a solemn, impressive effect upon those outside. The same was realized in the first private execution within Newgate, that of Alexander Mackay, who murdered his mistress at Norton Folgate by beating her with a rolling-pin and furnace-rake, and who expiated his crime on the 8th September, 1868. A more marked change from the old scene can hardly be conceived. Instead of the roar of the brutalized crowd, the officials spoke in whispers; there was but little moving to and fro. Almost absolute silence prevailed until the great bell began to toll its deep note, and broke the stillness with its regular and monotonous clangour, and the ordinary, in a voice trembling with emotion, read the burial service aloud. Mackay's fortitude, which had been great, broke down at the supreme moment before the horror of the stillness, the awful impressiveness of the scene in which he was the principal actor. No time was lost in carrying out the dread ceremony; but it was not completed without some of the officials turning sick, and the moment it was over, all who could were glad to escape from the last act of the ghastly drama at which they had assisted.

Private executions at their first introduction were not popular with the Newgate officials, and for intelligible reasons. The change added greatly to the responsibilities of the governor and his subordinates. Hitherto the public had seemed to assist at the ceremony; the moment too that the condemned man had passed through the debtors' door on to the scaffold the prison had done with him, and the great outside world shared in the completion of the sacrifice. This feeling was the stronger because all the ghastly paraphernalia, the gallows itself and the process of erecting and removing it, rested with the city architect, and not with the prison officials. Moreover, after the execution, under the old system, the latter had only to receive the body for burial after it had been cut down by the hangman, and placed decently in a shell by the workmen who removed the gallows. Under the new system the whole of the arrangements from first to last fell upon the officers. It was they who formed the chief part of the small select group of spectators; upon them devolved the painful duty of cutting down the body and preparing for the inquest. All that the hangman, whoever he may be, does under the new regime is to unhook the halter and remove the pinioning straps. The interment in a shell filled with quicklime in the passage-way leading to the Old Bailey is also a part of the duty of the prison officials. This strange burial-ground is one of the most ghastly of the remaining "sights" in Newgate. It was sometimes used as an exercising yard, and for the greater security of prisoners it is roofed in with iron bars, which gives it, at least overhead, the aspect of a huge cage. Underfoot and upon the walls roughly cut into the stones, are single initial letters, the brief epitaphs of those who lie below. As this burial-ground leads to the adjacent Central Criminal Court, accused murderers, on going to and returning from trial, literally walked over what, in case of conviction, would be their own graves.

The older officers, with several of whom I have conversed, have thus had unusual opportunities of watching the demeanour of murderers both before trial and after sentence. All, as a rule, unless poignant remorse has brought a desire to court their richly-merited retribution, are buoyed up with hope to the last. There is always the chance of a flaw in the indictment, of a missing witness, or extenuating circumstances. Even when in the condemned cell, with a shameful death within measurable distance, many cling still to life, expecting much from the intercession of friends or the humanitarianism of the age. All almost without exception sleep soundly at night, except the first after sentence, when the first shock of the verdict and the solemn notification of the impending blow keeps nearly all awake, or at least disturbs their night's rest. But the uneasiness soon wears off. The second night sleep comes readily, and is sound; many of the most abandoned murderers snore peacefully their eight hours, even on the night immediately preceding execution. All too have a fairly good appetite, and eat with relish up to the last moment. A few go further, and are almost gluttonous. Giovanni Lanni, the Italian boy who murdered a Frenchwoman in the Haymarket, and was arrested on board ship just as he was about to leave the country, had a little spare cash, which he devoted entirely to the purchase of extra food. He ate constantly and voraciously after sentence, as though eager to cram as many meals as possible into the few hours still left him to live. Jeffrey, who murdered his own child, an infant of six, by hanging him in a cellar in Seven Dials, called for a roast duck directly he entered the condemned cell. The request was not granted, as the old custom of allowing capital convicts whatever they asked for in the way of food has not been the rule in Newgate. The diet of the condemned is the ordinary diet of the prison, but to which additions are sometimes made, chiefly of stimulants, if deemed necessary, by the medical officer of the gaol. The craving for tobacco which so dominates the habitual smoker often leads the convicted to plead hard for a last smoke. As a special favour Wainwright was allowed a cigar the night before execution, which he smoked in the prison yard, walking up and down with the governor, Mr. Sydney Smith.

Wainwright's demeanour was one of reckless effrontery steadily maintained to the last. His conversation turned always upon his influence over the weaker sex, and the extraordinary success he had achieved. No woman could resist him, he calmly assured Mr. Smith that night as they walked together, and he recounted his villainies one by one. His effrontery was only outdone by his cool contempt for the consolations of religion. The man who had made a pious life a cloak for his misdeeds, the once exemplary young man and indefatigable Sunday school teacher, went impenitent to the gallows. The only sign of feeling he showed was in asking to be allowed to choose the hymns on the Sunday the condemned sermon was preached in the prison chapel, and this was probably only that he might hear the singing of a lady with a magnificent voice who generally attended the prison services. During the singing of these hymns Wainwright fainted, but whether from real emotion or the desire to make a sensation was never exactly known. On the fatal morning he came gaily out of his cell, nodded pleasantly to the governor, who stood just opposite, and then walked briskly towards the execution shed, smiling as he went along. There was a smile on his face when it was last seen, and just as the terrible white cap was drawn over it. Wainwright's execution was within the gaol, but only nominally private. No less than sixty-seven persons were present, admitted by special permission of the sheriff. Rumour even went so far as to assert that among the spectators were several women, disguised in male habiliments; but the story was never substantiated, and we may hope that it rested only on the idle gossip of the day.

Many, like Wainwright, were calm and imperturbable throughout their trying ordeal. Catherine Wilson, the poisoner, was reserved and reticent to the last, expressing no contrition, but also no fear—a tall, gaunt, repulsive-looking woman, who no more shrank from cowardly, secret crimes than from the penalty they entailed. Kate Webster, who was tried at the Central Criminal Court, and passed through Newgate, although she suffered at Wandsworth, is remembered at the former prison as a defiant, brutal creature who showed no remorse, but was subject to fits of ungovernable passion, when she broke out into the most appalling language. The man Marley displayed fortitude of a less repulsive kind. He acknowledged his guilt from the first. When the sheriff offered him counsel for his defence, he declined, saying he wished to make none—"the witnesses for the prosecution spoke the truth." During the trial and after sentence he remained perfectly cool and collected. When visited one day in the condemned cell, just as St. Sepulchre's clock was striking, he looked up and said laughingly, "Go along, clock; come along, gallows." He tripped up the chapel-stairs to hear the condemned sermon, and came out with cheerful alacrity on the morning he was to die.

Some condemned convicts converse but little with the warders who have them unceasingly in charge. Others talk freely enough on various topics, but principally upon their own cases. When vanity is strongly developed there is the keen anxiety to hear what is being said about them outside. One was vexed to think that his victims had a finer funeral than he would have. The only subject another showed any interest in was the theatres and the new pieces that were being produced. A third, Christian Sattler, laughed and jested with the officers about "Jack Ketch," who, through the postponement of the execution, would lose his Christmas dinner. When they brought in the two watchers to relieve guard one night, Sattler said, "Two fresh men! May I speak to them? Yes! I must caution you," he went on to the warders, "not to go to sleep, or I shall be off through that little hole," pointing to an aperture for ventilating the cell. On the morning of execution he asked how far it was to the gallows, and was told it was quite close. "Then I shall not wear my coat," he cried; "Jack Ketch shall not have it," being under the erroneous impression that the convict's clothes were still the executioner's perquisite.

Often the convicts give way to despair. They are too closely watched to be allowed to do themselves much mischief, or suicides would probably be more frequent. But it is neither easy to obtain the instruments of self-destruction nor to elude the vigilance of their guard. Miller, the Chelsea murderer, who packed his victim's body in a box, and tried to send it by parcels delivery, tried to kill himself, but ineffectively, by running his head against his cell wall. A few other cases of the kind have occurred, but they have been rare of late years, whether in Newgate or elsewhere.

The crime of poisoning has always been viewed with peculiar loathing and terror in this country. It will be remembered that as far back as the reign of Henry VIII a new and most cruel penalty was devised for the punishment of the Bishop of Rochester's cook, who had poisoned his master and many of his dependents. Sir Thomas Overbury was undoubtedly poisoned by Lord Rochester in the reign of James I, and it is hinted that James himself nearly fell a victim to a nefarious attempt of the Duke of Buckingham. But secret poisoning on a wholesale scale such as was practised in Italy and France was happily never popularized in England. The well-known and lethal aqua Toffania, so called after its inventress, a Roman woman named Toffania, and which was so widely adopted by ladies anxious to get rid of their husbands, was never introduced into this country. Its admission was probably checked by the increased vigilance at the custom houses, the necessity for which was urged by Mr. Addison, when Secretary of State, in 1717. The cases of poisoning in the British calendars are rare, nor indeed was the guilt of the accused always clearly established. It is quite possible that Catherine Blandy, who poisoned her father at the instigation of her lover, was ignorant of the destructive character of the powders, probably arsenic, which she administered. Captain Donellan, who was convicted of poisoning his brother-in-law, Sir Theodosius Broughton, and executed for it, would probably have had the benefit in these days of the doubts raised at his trial. A third case, more especially interesting to us as having passed through Newgate, was that of Eliza Fenning, who was convicted of an attempt to poison a whole family by putting arsenic in the dumplings she had prepared for them. The charge rested entirely on circumstantial evidence, and as Fenning, although convicted and executed, protested her innocence in the most solemn manner to the last, the justice of the sentence was doubted at the time. Yet it was clearly proved that the dumplings contained arsenic, that she, and she alone, had made the dough, that arsenic was within her reach in the house, that she had had a quarrel with her mistress, and that the latter with all others who tasted the dumplings were similarly attacked, although no one died.

The crime of poisoning is essentially one which will be most prevalent in a high state of civilization, when the spread of scientific knowledge places nefarious means at the disposal of many, instead of limiting them, as in the days of the Borgias and Brinvilliers, to the specially informed and unscrupulously powerful few. The first intimation conveyed to society of the new terror which threatened it was in the arrest and arraignment of William Palmer, a medical practitioner, charged with doing to death persons who relied upon his professional skill. The case contained elements of much uncertainty, and yet it was so essential to the interests and the due protection of the public that the fullest and fairest inquiry should be made, that the trial was transferred to the Central Criminal Court, under the authority of an Act passed for this purpose, known as the Trial of Offences Act, and sometimes as Lord Campbell's Act. That the administration of justice should never be interfered with by local prejudice or local feeling is obviously of paramount importance, and the powers granted by this Act have been frequently put in practice since. The trial of Catherine Winsor, the baby farmer, was thus brought to the Central Criminal Court from Exeter assizes, and that of the Stauntons from Maidstone.

Palmer's trial caused the most intense excitement. The direful suspicions which surrounded the case filled the whole country with uneasiness and misgiving, and the deepest anxiety was felt that the crime, if crime there had been, should be brought home to its perpetrator. The Central Criminal Court was crowded to suffocation. Great personages occupied seats upon the bench; the rest of the available space was allotted by ticket, to secure which the greatest influence was necessary. People came to stare at the supposed cold-blooded prisoner; with morbid curiosity to scan his features and watch his demeanour through the shifting, nicely-balanced phases of his protracted trial. Palmer, who was only thirty-one at the time of his trial, was in appearance short and stout, with a round head covered rather scantily with light sandy hair. His skin was extraordinarily fair, his cheeks fresh and ruddy; altogether his face, though commonplace, was not exactly ugly; there was certainly nothing in it which indicated cruel cunning or deliberate truculence. His features were not careworn, but rather set, and he looked older than his age. Throughout his trial he preserved an impassive countenance, but he clearly took a deep interest in all that passed. Although the strain lasted fourteen days, he showed no signs of exhaustion, either physical or mental. On returning to gaol each day he talked freely and without reserve to the warders in charge of him, chiefly on incidents in the day's proceedings. He was confident to the very last that it would be impossible to find him guilty; even after sentence, and until within a few hours of execution, he was buoyed up with the hope of reprieve. The conviction that he would escape had taken so firm a hold of him, that he steadily refused to confess his guilt lest it should militate against his chances. In the condemned cell he frequently repeated, "I go to my death a murdered man." He made no distinct admissions even on the scaffold; but when the chaplain at the last moment exhorted him to confess, he made use of the remarkable words, "If it is necessary for my soul's sake to confess this murder (that of Cook, for which he was tried and sentenced to death), I ought also to confess the others: I mean my wife and my brother's." Yet he was silent when specifically pressed to confess that he had killed his wife and his brother.

Palmer was ably defended, but the weight of evidence was clearly with the prosecution, led by Sir Alexander Cockburn. A government prosecution was instituted, and Palmer was brought to Newgate for trial at the Central Criminal Court. There was not much reserve about him when there. He frequently declared before and during the trial that it would be impossible to find him guilty. He never actually said that he was not guilty, but he was confident he would not be convicted. He relied on the absence of the strychnia. But the chain of circumstantial evidence was strong enough to satisfy the jury, who agreed to their verdict in an hour. At the last moment Palmer tossed a bit of paper over to his counsel, on which he had written, "I think there will be a verdict of 'Not' Guilty." Even after the death sentence had been passed upon him he clung to the hope that the Government would grant him a reprieve. To the last, therefore, he played the part of a man wrongfully convicted, and did not abandon hope even when the high sheriff had told him there was no possibility of a reprieve, within a few hours of execution. He suffered at Stafford in front of the gaol.

Palmer speedily found imitators. Within a few weeks occurred the Leeds poisoning case, in which the murderer undoubtedly was inspired by the facts made public at Palmer's trial. Dove, a fiendish brute, found from the evidence in that case that he could kill his wife, whom he hated, with exquisite torture, and with a poison that would leave, as he thought, no trace. In the latter hope he was happily disappointed. But as this case is beyond my subject, I merely mention it as one of the group already referred to. Three years later came the case of Dr. Smethurst, presenting still greater features of resemblance with Palmer's, for both were medical men, and both raised difficult questions of medical jurisprudence. In both the jury had no doubt as to the guilt of the accused, only in Smethurst's case the then Home Secretary, Sir George Cornewall Lewis, could not divest his mind of serious doubt, of which the murderer got the full benefit. Smethurst's escape may have influenced the jury in the Poplar poisoning case, which followed close on its heels, although in that the verdict of "Not Guilty" was excusable, as the evidence was entirely circumstantial. There was no convincing proof that the accused had administered the poison, although beyond question that poison had occasioned the death.

Catherine Wilson was a female poisoner who did business wholesale. She was tried in April, 1862, on suspicion of having attempted to poison a neighbour with oil of vitriol. The circumstances were strange. Mrs. Wilson had gone to the chemist's for medicine, and on her return had administered a dose of something which burned the mouth badly, but did not prove fatal.

She was acquitted on this charge, but other suspicious facts cropped up while she was in Newgate. It appeared that several persons with whom she was intimate had succumbed suddenly. In all cases the symptoms were much the same, vomiting, violent retching, purging, such as are visible in cholera, and all dated from the time when she knew a young man named Dixon, who had been in the habit of taking colchicum for rheumatism. Mrs. Wilson heard then casually from a medical man that it was a very dangerous medicine, and she profited by what she had heard. Soon afterwards Dixon died, showing all the symptoms already described. A little later a friend, Mrs. Atkinson, came to London from Westmoreland, and stayed in Mrs. Wilson's house. She was in good health on leaving home, and had with her a large sum of money. While with Mrs. Wilson she became suddenly and alarmingly ill, and died in great agony. Her husband, who came up to town, would not allow a post-mortem, and again Mrs. Wilson escaped. Mrs. Atkinson's symptoms had been the same as Dixon's. Then Mrs. Wilson went to live with a man named Taylor, who was presently attacked in the same way as the others, but, thanks to the prompt administration of remedies, he recovered. After this came the charge of administering oil of vitriol, which failed, as has been described. Last of all Mrs. Wilson poisoned her landlady, Mrs. Soames, under precisely the same conditions as the foregoing.

Here, however, the evidence was strong and sufficient. It was proved that Mrs. Wilson had given Mrs. Soames something peculiar to drink, that immediately afterwards Mrs. Soames was taken ill with vomiting and purging, and that Mrs. Wilson administered the same medicine again and again. The last time Mrs. Soames showed great reluctance to take it, but Wilson said it would certainly do her good. This mysterious medicine Wilson kept carefully locked up, and allowed no one to see it, but its nature was betrayed when this last victim also died. The first post-mortem indicated death from natural causes, but a more careful investigation attributed it beyond doubt to over-doses of colchicum. Dr. Alfred Taylor, the great authority and writer on medical jurisprudence, corroborated this, and in his evidence on the trial fairly electrified the court by declaring it his opinion that many deaths, supposed to be from cholera, were really due to poison. This fact was referred to by the judge in his summing up, who said that he feared it was only too true that secret poisoning was at that time very rife in the metropolis. Wilson was duly sentenced to death, and suffered impenitent, hardened, and without any confession of her guilt.

Although murder by insidious methods had become more common, cases where violence of the most deadly and determined kind was offered had not quite disappeared. Two cases of this class are of the most interest; one accompanied with piracy on the high seas, the other perpetrated in a railway-carriage, and showing the promptitude with which criminals accept and utilize altered conditions of life, more particularly as regards locomotion.

The first case was that of the *Flowery Land*, which left London for Singapore on the 28th July, 1863, with a cargo of wine and other goods. Her captain was John Smith; the first and second mates, Karswell and Taffir; there were two other Englishmen on board, and the rest of the crew were a polyglot lot, most of them, as was proved by their subsequent acts, blackguards of the deepest dye. Six were Spaniards, or rather natives of Manila, and men of colour; one was a Greek, another a Turk; there were also a Frenchman, a Norwegian (the carpenter), three Chinamen, a "Slavonian," and a black on board. Navigation and discipline could not be easy with such a nondescript crew. The captain was kindly but somewhat intemperate, the first mate a man of some determination, and punishment such as rope's-ending and tying to the bulwarks had to be applied to get the work properly done. The six Spaniards, the Greek, and the Turk were in the same watch, eight truculent and reckless scoundrels, who, brooding over their fancied wrongs, and burning for revenge, hatched amongst them a plot to murder their officers and seize the ship. The mutiny was organized with great secrecy, and broke out most unexpectedly in the middle of the night. A simultaneous attack was made upon the captain and the first mate. The latter had the watch on deck. One half of the mutineers fell upon him unawares with handspikes and capstan-bars. He was struck down, imploring mercy, but they beat him about the head and face till every feature was obliterated, and then, still living, flung him into the sea. Meanwhile the captain, roused from his berth, came out of the cabin, was caught near the "companion" by the rest of the mutineers, and promptly despatched with daggers. His body was found lying in a pool of blood in a night-dress, stabbed over and over again in the left side. The captain's brother, a passenger on board the *Flowery Land*, was also stabbed to death and his body thrown overboard.

The second mate, who had heard the hammering of the capstan-bars and the handspikes, with the first mate's and captain's agonized cries, had come out, verified the murderers, and then shut himself up in his cabin. He was soon summoned on deck, but as he would not move, the mutineers came down and stood in a circle round his berth. Leon, or Lyons, who spoke English, when asked said they would spare his life if he would navigate the ship for them to the River Plate or Buenos Ayres. Taffir agreed, but constantly went in fear of his life for the remainder of the voyage; and although the mutineers spared him, they ill-treated the Chinamen, and cut one badly with knives. Immediately after the murder, cases of champagne, which formed part of the cargo, were brought on deck and emptied; the captain's cabin ransacked, his money and clothes divided amongst the mutineers, as well as much of the merchandise on board. Leon wished to make every one on board share and share alike, so as to implicate the innocent with the guilty; but Vartos, or Watto, the Turk, would not allow any but the eight mutineers to have anything. The murders were perpetrated on the 10th September, and the ship continued her voyage for nearly three weeks, meeting and speaking one ship only. On the 2nd October they sighted land, ten miles distant; the mutineers took command of the ship, put her about till nightfall, by which time they had scuttled her, got out the boats, and all left the ship. The rest of the crew were also permitted to embark, except the Chinamen, one of whom was thrown into the water and drowned, while the other two were left to go down in the ship, and were seen clinging to the tops until the waters closed over them.

The boats reached the shore on the 4th October. Leon had prepared a plausible tale to the effect that they belonged to an American ship from Peru bound to Bordeaux, which had foundered at sea; that they had been in the boats five days and nights, but that the captain and others had been lost. The place at which they landed was not far from the entrance to the River Plate. A farmer took them in for the night, and drove them next day to Rocha, a place north of Maldonado. Taffir, the mate, finding there was a man who could speak English at another place twenty miles off, repaired there secretly, and so gave information to the Brazilian authorities. The mutineers were arrested, the case inquired into by a naval court-martial, and the prisoners eventually surrendered to the British authorities, brought to England, and lodged in Newgate. Their trial followed at the Central Criminal Court. Eight were arraigned at the same time: six Spaniards; Leon, Lopez, Blanco, Duranno, Santos, and Marsolino; Vartos, a Turk, and Carlos, a Greek. Seven were found guilty of murder on the high seas, and one, Carlos, acquitted. Two of the seven, Santos and Marsolino, were reprieved, and their sentences commuted to penal servitude for life; the remaining five were executed in one batch. They were an abject, miserable crew, cowards at heart; but some, especially Lopez, continued bloodthirsty to the last. Lopez took a violent dislike to the officer of the ward in charge of them, and often expressed a keen desire to do for him. They none of them spoke much English except Leon, commonly called Lyons. After condemnation, as the rules now kept capital convicts strictly apart, they could not be lodged in the two condemned cells, and they were each kept in an ordinary separate cell of the newly-constructed block, with the "traps," or square openings in the cell door, let down. A full view of them was thus at all times obtainable by the officers who, without intermission, day and night patrolled the ward. On the morning of execution the noise of fixing the gallows in the street outside awoke one or two of them. Lyons asked the time, and was told it was only five. "Ah!" he remarked, "they will have to wait for us then till eight." Lopez was more talkative. When the warder went in to call him he asked for his clothes. He was told he would have to wear his own. "Not give clothes? In Russia, Italy, always give chaps clothes." Then he wanted to know when the policemen would arrive, and was told none would come. "The soldiers then?" No soldiers either. "What, you not afraid let us go all by ourselves? Not so in Russia or Spain." The convicts were pinioned one by one and sent singly out to the gallows. As the first to appear would have some time to wait for his fellows, a difficult and painful ordeal, the seemingly most courageous was selected to lead the way. This was Duranno; but the sight of the heaving mass of uplifted, impassioned faces was too much for his nerves, and he so nearly fainted that he had to be seated in a chair. The execution went off without mishap.

In July, 1864, occurred the murder of Mr. Briggs, a gentleman advanced in years and chief clerk in Robarts' bank. As the circumstances under which it was perpetrated were somewhat novel,[274:1] and as some time elapsed before the discovery and apprehension of the supposed murderer, the public mind was greatly agitated by the affair for several months. The story of the murder must be pretty familiar to most of my readers. Mr. Briggs left the bank one afternoon as usual, dined with his daughter at Peckham, then returned to the city to take the train from Fenchurch Street home, travelling by the North London Railway. He lived at Hackney, but he never reached it alive. When the train arrived at Hackney station, a passenger who was about to enter one of the carriages found the cushions soaked with blood. Inside the carriage was a hat, a walking-stick, and a small black leather bag. About the same time a body was discovered on the line near the railway-bridge by Victoria Park. It was that of an aged man, whose head had been battered in by a life-preserver. There was a deep wound just over the ear, the skull was fractured, and there were several other blows and wounds on the head. Strange to say, the unfortunate man was not yet dead, and he actually survived more than four-and-twenty hours. His identity was established by a bundle of letters in his pocket, which bore his full address: "T. Briggs, Esq., Robarts & Co., Lombard Street."

The friends of Mr. Briggs were communicated with, and it was ascertained that when he left home the morning of the murderous attack, he wore gold-rimmed eye-glasses and a gold watch and chain. The stick and bag were his, but not the hat. A desperate and deadly struggle must have taken place in the carriage, and the stain of a bloody hand marked the door. The facts of the murder and its object, robbery, were thus conclusively proved. It was also easily established that the hat found in the carriage had been bought at Walker's, a hatter's in Crawford Street, Marylebone; while within a few days Mr. Briggs' gold chain was traced to a jeweller's in Cheapside, Mr. Death, who had given another in exchange for it to a man supposed to be a foreigner. More precise clues to the murderer were not long wanting; indeed the readiness with which they were produced and followed up showed how greatly the publicity and wide dissemination of the news regarding murder facilitate the detection of crime. In little more than a week a cabman came forward and voluntarily made a statement which at once drew suspicion to a German, Franz Müller, who had been a lodger of his. Müller had given the cabman's little daughter a jeweller's cardboard box bearing the name of Mr. Death. A photograph of Müller shown the jeweller was identified as the likeness of the man who had exchanged Mr. Briggs' chain. Last of all, the cabman swore that he had bought the very hat found in the carriage for Müller at the hatter's, Walker's of Crawford Street.

This fixed the crime pretty certainly upon Müller, who had already left the country, thus increasing the suspicion under which he lay. There was no mystery about his departure; he had gone to Canada by the *Victoria* sailing ship, starting from the London docks, and bound to New York. Directly the foregoing facts were established, a couple of detective officers, armed with a warrant to arrest Müller, and accompanied by Mr. Death the jeweller and the cabman, went down to Liverpool and took the first steamer across the Atlantic. This was the *City of Manchester*, which was expected to arrive some days before the *Victoria*, and did so. The officers went on board the *Victoria* at once, Müller was identified by Mr. Death, and the arrest was made. In searching the prisoner's box, Mr. Briggs' watch was found wrapped up in a piece of leather, and Müller at the time of his capture was actually wearing Mr. Briggs' hat, cut down and somewhat altered. The prisoner was forthwith extradited and sent back to England, which he reached with his escort on the 17th September the same year. His trial followed at the next sessions of the Central Criminal Court, and ended in his conviction. The case was one of circumstantial evidence, but, as Sir Robert Collyer, the Solicitor-General, pointed out, it was the strongest circumstantial evidence which had ever been brought forward in a murder case. It was really evidence of facts which could not be controverted or explained away. There was the prisoner's poverty, his inability to account for himself on the night of the murder, and his possession of the property of the murdered man. An alibi was set up for the defence, but not well substantiated, and the jury without hesitation returned a verdict of guilty.

Müller protested after sentence of death had been passed upon him that he had been convicted on a false statement of facts. He adhered to this almost to the very last. His case had been warmly espoused by the Society for the Protection of Germans in this country, and powerful influence was exerted both here and abroad to obtain a reprieve. Müller knew that any confession would ruin his chances of escape. His arguments were specious and evasive when pressed to confess. "Why should man confess to man?" he replied; "man cannot forgive man, only God can do so. Man is therefore only accountable to God." But on the gallows, when the cap was over his eyes and the rope had been adjusted round his neck, and within a second of the moment when he would be launched into eternity, he whispered in the ear of the German pastor who attended him on the scaffold, "I did it." While in the condemned cell he conversed freely with the warders in broken English or through an interpreter. He is described as not a bad-looking man, with a square German type of face, blue eyes which were generally half closed, and very fair hair. He was short in stature, his legs were light for the upper part of his body, which was powerful, almost herculean. It is generally supposed that he committed the murder under a sudden access of covetousness and greed. He saw Mr. Briggs' watch-chain, and followed him instantly into the carriage, determined to have it at all costs.

An interesting case is that of old Dr. Watson, the headmaster of Stockwell Grammar School, who escaped the final retribution of death because, as he pleaded for himself: "In a fit of fury I have killed my wife. Often and often have I endeavoured to restrain myself but my rage overcame me and I struck her down. Her body will be found in the little room off the library. I hope she will be buried as becomes a lady of birth and position. She is an Irish lady and her name is Anne." Here were unmistakably signs of feeble intellect, and yet when the deed was done he was sufficiently sensible and self-possessed to make a cunning attempt to conceal his crime. His great desire, as so often happens with murderers, was to dispose of the chief evidence of his guilt and he was quite cool and collected when he gave his orders to a packing-case maker to prepare him a large chest. "And I want it done sharp; it must be air and water tight, for it is to go by rail." Then he seems to have broken down and bought poison which failed of effect and led to the discovery of the crime.

Henry Wainwright's murder of Harriet Lane was a crime on a parity with many others of earlier date. It was a curious instance of how "murder will out," and how the devices employed to hide the crime help really to expose it. Too much chloride of lime had been employed to consume the buried corpse with the result that the body was preserved instead of destroyed. Again, a mere chance led to the discovery; the carelessness of the murderer when he had exhumed the body for removal to some safer place, in entrusting the parcel to a stranger's hands who was curious as to its contents. The plea set up by the accused that the girl had committed suicide led to the shrewd remark of the judge, Chief Justice Goulbourne, that it was very unusual for suicides to bury themselves after death. Henry Wainwright's was one of the last executions at Newgate.

A case, almost unique, may be quoted of a nearly successful attempt to interfere with the course of justice by means of a forged order of pardon. A convict on the point of execution, a man named Shurety, was actually in the hangman's hands when a letter was brought to the governor of Newgate purporting to come from the Home Office and signed "A. F. Liddell," then Under-secretary of State, countermanding the execution. The signature was so cleverly copied that it seemed genuine, but a closer examination of the letter, envelope and seal satisfied the authorities that the document was spurious and they took upon themselves to send Shurety to the gallows. A couple of months later the forgery was brought home to a surgeon, Mr. Caleb C. Whiteford, who had interested himself in the case and having failed to save the man by lawful means had adopted this course, which brought upon him a sentence of fine and imprisonment. Another curious case was the utter discomfiture of certain ultra-sentimentalists who had laboured strenuously to obtain a pardon for a Jew, Israel Lipski, alleged to have been wrongly convicted. Great excitement prevailed while he lay awaiting execution; numerous petitions were addressed to the Home Secretary, and his steadfast refusal to extend mercy was hysterically denounced by a section of the Press. Just when it was still asserted that judicial murder was on the point of being perpetrated, the convict made full confession of his crime and the ill-advised action of these busybodies was very properly overthrown. One or two more cases must serve to complete the list of the last great crimes expiated in Newgate. Mrs. Pearcey, who murdered her friend Mrs. Hogg, no doubt allowed her temper to get the better of her and what was at first a small quarrel unhappily degenerated into a murderous attack. The circumstances of the crime were commonplace; the special interest was in the method of removing the murdered remains. Mrs. Hogg's body with the throat cut had been found on Hampstead Heath and shortly afterwards her infant child was found dead in close proximity. It came out in the course of inquiry that Mrs. Pearcey had wheeled a perambulator containing the dead bodies all the way from St. John's Wood to Hampstead.

But for the lucky chance which so often assists the detection of great crimes, the Muswell Hill murder would hardly have been brought home to its perpetrators. This was a burglary which cost the life of the unfortunate victim, a Mr. Henry Smith, an aged gentleman who lived alone in a small villa on Muswell Hill, one of the northern suburbs of London. He was a man of some means who was weak enough to keep his cash receipts for rents and dividends in his own safe at home. He was a tall stout man of active habits and fairly robust health who "did for himself," rising early, cleaning his house, cooking his food and living his own simple life. His habits were watched and they marked him down as open to attack and robbery. One morning his gardener, the only servant he employed, and who lived away from the house, arrived as usual to find the premises still locked up. There were unmistakable signs that a forcible entry had been made and a wire connected with an alarm gun behind the house had been disconnected. Calling upon the neighbours for assistance, the gardener entered the house and saw Mr. Smith's body lying lifeless on the floor. The safe stood open and had been evidently rifled;

drawers had been pulled out and a tin box emptied. The murder had been committed with very brutal violence as the state of the body amply testified. Various small clues were forthcoming; a bull's eye lantern, two pocket knives upon the floor near the deceased and some bread and cheese which the murderers had been consuming after the deed. There were footprints in the garden leading down into the woods back of the house. Two sets of footprints, one of large boots with a very broad tread and no nails, the other of smaller boots with pointed toes. The footprints ended at the garden fence where there were many marks and scratches to show that someone had climbed over. A small tobacco box was also picked up on the footpath leading to the wood, the property of someone who did not live at the villa, for neither the murdered man nor the gardener were in the habit of smoking.

It is customary with the police in cases of this gravity to search their records and ascertain what known offenders likely to be guilty of such a crime were then at large. Two ex-convicts, Albert Milsom and Henry Fowler, stood upon the list and at once attracted the attention of the police as habitual criminals addicted to burglary, but there was no specific evidence against them until suspicion was raised by a young lady who resided near Muswell Hill. She thought it her duty to inform the police that she had been accosted by two men, a little before the murder, who had made many inquiries about the woods behind Mr. Smith's house. Another lady had seen the same man on the very day of the murder walking in a neighbouring lane. This was sufficient to cause inquiry to be made for the two men in question who were soon identified as the above mentioned Milsom and Fowler. Suspicion deepened when it became known that after the day of the murder they were flush of money and had bought new clothes. Then a damaging fact turned up when the bull's eye lantern picked up on the scene of the crime was claimed by Milsom's brother-in-law as his property. He proved his ownership by pointing out changes he had made in it and further that it had been abstracted from him some little time before the murder, and that the next time he saw it was in the hands of the police. The same lad recognized the tobacco box as one that Albert Milsom constantly used.

The next step was to "run in" the two men so strongly suspected. They were "wanted" for some weeks and although they seem to have still hung about London it was believed they had gone abroad. Towards the end of February they left for Liverpool and then moved south to Cardiff, where they joined forces with an itinerant showman having bought a share in his business. They moved to and fro in South Wales and then worked back to Chippenham and Bath where the police, ever hot on their track, came upon them and captured them after a desperate struggle. Fowler was a strong man of large frame and he fought like a tiger but was knocked on the head with the butt end of a revolver and overpowered. He owed his confederate Milsom a deep grudge and on more than one occasion made a murderous attempt on his life, once in the exercising yard at Holloway while awaiting trial, an affair which the present writer myself witnessed. The two men were walking in a circle some distance apart, but Fowler ran after him and was only prevented by the officers from doing him serious mischief. Again at the Old Bailey when the jury had retired to consider their verdict, Fowler jumped out of the dock and attacked his companion but was restrained in time. Milsom had enraged him by making full confession of the murder and the manner in which it had been committed. Fowler, he said, had done the deed alone but had bitterly upbraided Milsom for giving no assistance. Both criminals were executed in Newgate.

The last great case of fraud upon the Bank of England will fitly find a place in the later criminal records of Newgate. This was the well and astutely devised plot of the brothers Bidwell, assisted by Macdonell and Noyes, all of them citizens of the United States, by which the bank lost upwards of £100,000. The commercial experience of these clever rogues was cosmopolitan. Their operations were no less world-wide. In 1871 they crossed the Channel, and by means of forged letters of credit and introduction from London, obtained large sums from continental banks in Berlin, Dresden, Bordeaux, Marseilles and Lyons. With this as capital they came back to England via Buenos Ayres, and Austin Bidwell opened a bona fide credit in the Burlington or West End Branch of the Bank of England, to which he was introduced by a well known tailor in Saville Row. After this the other conspirators travelled to obtain genuine bills and master the system of the leading houses at home and abroad. When all was ready, Bidwell first "refreshed his credit" at the Bank of England, as well as disarmed suspicion, by paying in a genuine bill of Messrs. Rothschilds' for £4,500 which was duly discounted. Then he explained to the bank manager that his transactions at Birmingham would shortly be very large, owing to the development of his business there in the alleged manufacture of Pullman cars. The ground thus cleared, the forgers poured in from Birmingham numbers of forged acceptances to the value of £102,217, all of which were discounted. The fraud was rendered possible by the absence of a check customary in the United States. There such bills would be sent to the drawer to be initialled, and the forgery would have been at once detected. It was the discovery of this flaw in the banking system which had encouraged the Americans to attempt this crime.

Time was clearly an important factor in the fraud, hence the bills were sent forward in quick succession. Long before they came to maturity the forgers hoped to be well beyond arrest. They had, moreover, sought to destroy all clue. The sums obtained by Bidwell in the name of "Warren" at the Bank of England were lodged at once by drafts to "Horton" another alias, in the

Continental Bank. For these cash was obtained in notes; the notes were exchanged by one of the conspirators for gold at the Bank of England and again the same day a second conspirator exchanged the gold for notes. But just as all promised well, the frauds were detected through the carelessness of the forgers. They had omitted to insert the dates in certain bills. The bills were sent as a matter of form to the drawer to have the date added, and the forgery was at once detected. Noyes was seized without difficulty, as it was a part of the scheme that he should act as the dupe, and remain on the spot in London till all the money was obtained. Through Noyes the rest of the conspirators were eventually apprehended. Very little if any of the ill-gotten proceeds, however, was ever recovered. Large sums as they were realized were transmitted to the United States and invested in various American securities, where probably the money still remains.

The prisoners, who were committed to Newgate for trial, had undoubtedly the command of large funds while there, and would have readily disbursed it to effect their enlargement. A plot was soon discovered, deep laid, and with many ramifications, by which some of the Newgate warders were to be bribed to allow the prisoners to escape from their cells at night. Certain friends of the prisoners were watched and found to be in communication with these warders, to whom it was said £100 apiece had been given down as the price of their infidelity. Further sums were to have been paid after the escape; and one warder admitted that he was to have £1,000 more paid to him and to be provided with a passage to Australia. The vigilance of the Newgate officials assisted by the city police, completely frustrated this plot. A second was nevertheless set on foot in which the plan of action was changed, and the freedom of the prisoners was to be obtained by means of a rescue from the dock during the trial. An increase of policemen on duty sufficed to prevent any attempt of this kind. Nor were these two abortive efforts all that were planned. A year or two after, when the prisoners were undergoing their life sentences of penal servitude, much uneasiness was caused at one of the convict prisons by information that bribery on a large scale was again at work amongst the officials. But extra precautions and close supervision have so far proved effectual and the prisoners were still in custody after a lapse of ten years.

The time came at length when the old City Gaol must fall in with the steady and persistent march towards prison reform. The movement had been initiated by the legislative and certain improvements were made imperative, notably that which recognized the unalterable principle that every individual should be confined separately and singly in one cell or apartment. Already steps had been taken and public moneys voted to construct a prison on the most approved plan to serve as a model for all. The result was Pentonville, erected in 1842 at a great outlay and on such intelligent lines that in due course it fulfilled its first aim and became a model for imitation. Pentonville has been universally adopted as the best form of building and its system the best contrived to effect the chief desiderata of a penal establishment, such as coercion, repression and reformation. It is to be seen to-day with small variation in almost every country of the world and is generally considered the best type of prison construction. In England, jurisdictions were ready to recognize their duties and responsibilities and fine prisons arose in the large provincial cities and wide areas of population, although others still lagged behind deterred by parsimony and the lack of public spirit. Newgate, the gaol of the richest corporation in the world, was one of the latter and an official report published in 1850 animadverted strongly on its still unsatisfactory condition.

Not much had been done to remedy the old defects; radical improvement was generally considered impossible. The great evil, however, had been sensibly diminished. There was no longer, or at worst but rarely, and for short periods, the same overcrowding. This was obviated by the frequent sessions of the Central Criminal Court, and the utilization of the two subsidiary prisons in Giltspur Street and Southwark. The prison population of Newgate was still subject to great fluctuations, but it seldom rose above two hundred and fifty or three hundred at the most crowded periods, or just before the sessional gaol delivery; and at its lowest it fell sometimes to fifty or sixty. These numbers would have still further decreased, and the gaol would have been almost empty, but for the misdemeanants who were still sent to Newgate at times on long terms of imprisonment, and for the transports, whom the Home Office was often, as of old, slow to remove. The old wards, day rooms and sleeping rooms combined, now seldom contained more than ten or a dozen occupants. Some sort of decorum was maintained in the day-time. Drinking and gaming, the indiscriminate visitation of friends, and the almost unlimited admission of extra food, had disappeared.

But reformation was only skin deep. Below the surface many of the old evils still rankled. There was as yet no control over the prisoners after locking-up time; which occurred in summer at eight, but in the winter months took place at dusk, and was often as early as four or five o'clock. The prisoners were still left to themselves till next morning's unlocking, and they spent some fourteen or fifteen hours in total darkness, and almost without check or control. The only attempt at supervision was exercised by the night watchman stationed on the leads, who might hear what went on inside. If any disturbance reached his ears, he reported the case to the governor, who next morning visited the ward in fault, and asked for the culprit. The enforcement of discipline depended upon the want of honour among thieves. Unless the guilty prisoner was given up, the whole ward was punished, either by the exclusion of visitors or the deprivation of fire, sharp tests which generally broke down the fidelity of the inmates of the ward to one another. Later on a more efficacious but still imperfect method of supervision was introduced. Iron cages, which are still to be seen in Newgate, were constructed on the landings, ensconced in which warders spent the night, on duty, and alert to watch the sleepers below, and check by remonstrance or threat of punishment all who broke the peace of the prison.

These disciplinary improvements were, however, only slowly and gradually introduced. Other changes affecting the condition and proper treatment of prisoners were not made until repeatedly urged and recommended. Thus the wards, which, as I have said, were left in complete darkness, were now to be lighted with gas; and after this most salutary addition, the personal superintendence of night officers, as already described, became possible. The rule became general as regards the prison dress; hitherto clothing had been issued only to such as were destitute or in rags, and all classes of prisoners, those for trial, and those sentenced for short terms or long, wore no distinguishing costume, although its use was admitted, not only for cleanliness, but as a badge of condition, and a security against escape. Renewed recommendations to provide employment resulted in the provision of a certain amount of oakum for picking, and one or two men were allowed to mend clothes and make shoes. The rules made by the Secretary of State were hung up in conspicuous parts of the prison; more officers were appointed, as the time of so many of those already on the staff was monopolized by attendance at the Central Criminal Court. Another custom which had led to disorder was abolished; prisoners who had been acquitted were not permitted to return to the prison to show their joy and receive the congratulations of their unfortunate fellows. The Corporation seems to have introduced these salutary changes without hesitation. It was less prompt apparently in dealing with structural alterations and improvements. Well-founded complaints had been made of the want of heating appliances in the gaol. The wards had open fires, but the separate cells were not warmed at all. It was long before a scheme for heating the whole prison with hot water pipes was accepted and introduced.

At last the authorities realized that all idea of reconstruction on proper lines was out of the question. It was imperative to begin at the beginning, select a sufficiently spacious piece of ground and erect a prison thereon, which from foundations to roofs should be in conformity with the newest ideas.

Now for the first time the Tuffnell estate in Holloway was mentioned. The Corporation owned lands there covering from nineteen to twenty acres. Why not move the city prison bodily into this more rural spot, with its purer air and greater breathing space? Eventually Holloway was decided upon as a site for the new city prison. The necessary preliminaries took some time, but the contracts for the new building were completed in 1849, when the works were commenced. The prison was to contain four hundred and four prisoners, and the estimated expenditure was £79,000. It was to accommodate all convicted prisoners sentenced to terms short of penal servitude, and after its completion the uses of Newgate were narrowed almost entirely to those of a prison of detention. It was intended, as far as possible, that no prisoner should find himself relegated to Newgate except when awaiting trial.

With the reduction of numbers to be accommodated, there was ample space in Newgate for its reconstruction on the most approved modern lines. In 1857 the erection of a wing or large block of cells was commenced within the original walls of the prison, and upon the north or male side. This block contained one hundred and thirty cells, embracing every modern improvement; it also contained eleven reception cells, six punishment cells, and a couple of cells for condemned criminals. This block was completed in 1859, after which the hitherto unavoidable and long-continued promiscuous association of prisoners came to an end. In 1861 a similar work was undertaken to provide separate cell accommodation for the female inmates of Newgate, and by the following year forty-seven new cells had been built on the most approved plan. During this reconstruction the female prisoners were lodged in Holloway, and when it was completed, both sides of the prison were brought into harmony with modern ideas. The old buildings were entirely disused, and the entire number of those at Newgate were kept constantly in separate confinement.

With the last re-edification of Newgate, a work executed some seven centuries after the first stone of the old gaol was laid, the architectural records of the prison end. Nothing much was done at Newgate in the way of building, outside or inside, after 1862. The Act for private executions led to the erection of the gallows shed in the exercising yard, and at the flank of the passage from the condemned cells. The first "glass house," or room in which prisoners could talk in private with their attorneys, and still be seen by the warder on the watch, had been constructed, and others were subsequently added. But no structural alterations were made from the date first quoted until in 1902 the prison ceased to exist as such.

A few words will suffice in closing the record of this old-world prison, which after seven centuries of existence has no longer a place in the heart of the great overgrown city. It has been crowded out, the space it occupied was far too limited and yet too valuable to remain the centre of Metropolitan criminal procedure. It was imperative that the famous assize court of the Old Bailey should be enlarged and the ground upon which the prison stood was urgently needed for extension. The chief prison authority, the State itself which had administered to the powers so long exercised by local jurisdiction, decided to remove the last vestige of prison business from the ancient site. A prison already standing in the suburb of Brixton was enlarged and appropriated to meet the purposes which Newgate had fulfilled almost to the last. For it continued until yesterday to serve as the last resting place of malefactors condemned to death. It was still the succursal of the assize court, sheltering the accused during the trial and holding them after conviction until they stood finally under the drop and the fatal bolt was drawn. But Newgate in 1882 ceased to be more than a temporary prison receiving lodgers about to take the last long journey from which no traveller returns, and in this way old Newgate continued to be associated with all capital offences in London.

Many pages might still be filled with painful stories often reproducing almost exactly the criminal episodes of the past and proving that there is literally nothing new under the sun. The latest Newgate records exhibited the same fatal consequences of overpowering greed, unappeasable rage, brutal passions uncontrolled; the same fierce thirst for vengeance; the same bitter jealousy, only to be assuaged in blood under the maddened impulse of minds on the borderland of insanity. Great crimes may be rarer nowadays, but they still present the same familiar features as of old, and will no doubt do so while the world lasts.

NOTE. Occasional references to the Tower have been made in the preceding chapters. Its history in full would be the history of England and far too extended for the scope of this work; therefore an outline only is given, with reference in brief to many important prisoners who were confined or suffered within its gloomy walls.

Great Court of the Tower of London

Ancient palace-citadel of London, and famous state prison, whose history began with William the Conqueror. The chief buildings of the group are the work of Norman kings and Henry III. Familiar as the place of durance and scene of death of many prisoners of royal blood and political importance.

FOOTNOTES:

[274:1] They have since been repeated, but accompanied by more premeditation, in the case of Lefroy, who murdered Mr. Gould in a first-class carriage on the Brighton line in 1881.

CHAPTER X
THE TOWER OF LONDON

Location—Traditions of ancient fortifications—William the Conqueror and Gundulf the Builder—Additions by other kings—The first prisoners—Royal tenants—Richard Duke of Gloucester and the "Two Little Princes"—Increase in number of prisoners during Tudor period—Anne Boleyn's two visits to the Tower—Another queen's fate—The "Nine Days' Queen" and her friends—Spanish influence fills the Tower—Sir Walter Raleigh—Lady Arabella Stuart—Executions grow fewer—Culloden—The last man beheaded in England—Present uses of the Tower.

On the north bank of the Thames, a half mile below London Bridge and just east of the old city of London, stands an irregular pile of buildings with walls, battlements and moat which fires the imagination, and grips the fancy as no other group in the world can do.

The Tower of London, in turn fortress, palace and prison—sometimes all three simultaneously—and now a storehouse and museum, has a continuous existence almost as long as England's history. Tradition says that the Britons had a stronghold here before Cæsar came; that the great Roman himself ordered the walls strengthened; that the Saxon kings held court on the site. Certainly excavations for various purposes made from time to time have revealed masonry and relics of all three periods.

The Tower as we have it to-day goes back only to the Norman kings. William the Conqueror's keen eye saw the advantage of this low hill and wished a fortress which should command the river and help to overawe the turbulent city to the west. Gundulf, a Benedictine monk, whom he had made Bishop of Rochester, and who had shown his ability by rebuilding the cathedral there, set to work in 1078 or 1079 on the keep, or White Tower.

This great building stands to-day his monument. The solid masonry walls twelve to sixteen feet thick enclose the vaults formerly used as torture chambers when occasion demanded, the main floor, the banqueting floor and the state floor. The chapel of St. John the Evangelist rises through two floors in the southeast corner, while the low towers at the four corners command the scene for miles. Old Gundulf built well, and completed also St. Peter's chapel and the Hall tower. The other towers with their connecting walls enclosing the Inner Ward were built later, many of them by Henry III. The Beauchamp tower, the Belfry, the Garden or Bloody tower, the Lantern, the Salt tower, the Broad Arrow tower, the Constable tower, the Martin tower, the Brick tower, the Flint tower, the Bowyer tower and the Develin tower, were all built in the wall for purposes of defence, but all have sheltered prisoners from time to time.

Within this Inner Ward, besides the buildings already named were royal apartments and a Great Hall of justice (long since destroyed), the mint, which remained until 1810, residences for officers, barracks, etc. Around all this was a second strong wall protected by other strong towers, which was planned and partially constructed by Henry III. Of these towers on the outer wall, St. Thomas' tower on the river—better known as the Traitors' Gate—is the most important. Under this tower prisoners were landed from the river. The space enclosed by the outer wall is about thirteen acres, and around all was a broad moat flooded from the Thames.

The importance of the Tower as a fortress diminished with the invention of gunpowder, but it continued to be used as a royal residence, at intervals, until the accession of Charles II. Here Henry III lived and planned great structures; during the wars of the Roses, York and Lancaster held court in turn; Henry VII schemed for greater wealth, and his son was led to defy the Pope while keeping a residence here.

But it is with the Tower as a prison that we are most concerned. The roll of the prisoners tells England's history. The petty intrigues of court favourites; the greatness or the meanness of kings; the struggle for power among great families; the truckling to foreign power which brought Raleigh to the block, and the great struggle for religious and political freedom are all set forth in the story of this great prison.

The first prisoner confined within the walls appears to have been Ralph Flambard, (the Firebrand), Bishop of Durham, who as treasurer of William the Conqueror had been forced to find the funds for old Gundulf's work. Hated by the commons for his exactions, he was taken into custody on the accession of Henry Beauclerc and was lodged in an upper room of the White tower, as yet unsurrounded by walls. He was well treated and allowed many privileges, but his efforts to secure his release were unsuccessful. One night in February, 1101, when he had caused all his guards to drink heavily of wine brought in at his expense, he drew a rope from one of the casks, tied it to the window sixty-five feet from the ground, and descended. Though the rope was short and he fell heavily, his servants were waiting, and he made good his escape to France, there to remain until forgiven and restored to his bishopric.

Another important early prisoner was the victim of King John's unlawful love, Maud Fitzwalter, the daughter of one of his powerful barons, who refused to grant his will. The coward king attempted to break her spirit by confinement in an uncomfortable cell, and banished her family. Bravely resisting the king's desires to the end, she died, perhaps by poison. Her father returned and placed himself at the head of that band of bishops and barons who compelled the king to sign the Great Charter at Runnymede.

Next we hear of the incarceration of six hundred Jews charged by Edward I with tampering with the coinage. The same king brought John de Baliol, king of Scotland, and David Bruce to the Tower in 1298, and William Wallace, the hero of Scotland, was imprisoned here in 1305 before his execution at Smithfield. During this reign also Griffin, Prince of Wales, who had been first confined by Henry III, attempted to escape by the same method which Flambard had used so successfully, but his cord, made from strips of his bed coverings, was too weak and his neck was broken by the fall.

During the unhappy reign of Edward II court was kept in the Tower with a splendour before unknown. Here the king's children were born, and here Roger Mortimer, although a captive, began the guilty intrigue with Queen Isabella which ended in disaster and disgrace for all.

More royal tenants appeared under Edward III. King David of Scotland was confined in 1347, and in 1358, after Poitiers, King John of France and his son joined the great number of French nobles whom the fortunes of war had brought hither. It was in the Tower also that Edward's unworthy grandson, Richard II, saw his favourite, Simon Burley, seized by the indignant nobles and finally taken to Tower Hill. It is said that this was the first public execution on Tower Hill, just north of the Tower itself. In the Tower also Sir John Oldcastle suffered, and the old walls saw Richard yield to Henry of Lancaster the crown which he was too weak to hold.

With the accession of Henry V the war with France was renewed and again many French nobles became tenants of the pile. One of them, Charles of Orleans, grandson of Charles V, is described by Shakespeare. Wounded and captured at Agincourt, the impossible ransom of 300,000 crowns was demanded by his unsuccessful rival, Henry V, who had failed to win the love of Isabella, widow of Richard II of England. Indeed Henry preferred that he remain a perpetual prisoner; and a prisoner he remained for twenty-five years, spending his time with his books and his verses, many addressed to his dead wife. Finally released, he married Mary of Cleves, and their son was Louis XII, who married Mary, the sister of Henry VIII of England.

With the Wars of the Roses, the records became more bloody, and the sanguinary tinge continues through the Tudor period. During the first period it was great house against great house, but during the Tudor period began the great struggle for political freedom, which at times seemed hopeless of attainment.

No figure so dominates the first period as the sinister, humpbacked brother of Edward IV, Richard, Duke of Gloucester, Richard III of England. His influence is felt in the sober history as well as in the plays of Shakespeare. He is said to have stabbed with his own hand the imbecile Henry VI, who had already at a previous time spent five years a prisoner in the Tower. Tradition persists that he drowned his brother the Duke of Clarence, in a butt of the latter's favourite wine. We know of his denunciation of Lord Hastings on charge of witchcraft and of the murder of that unhappy nobleman. We know that he kept Jane Shore, the mistress of his brother, in prison here until all her charms were faded.

But the mysterious disappearance of the two little princes has done most to damn his memory. As the result of the marriage with Elizabeth Woodville, Edward IV left two sons, Edward V, aged twelve, and Richard, aged eight. Gloucester was Protector but with diabolical cunning threw doubt upon the legitimacy of the boys placed under his charge. They were confided to Sir John Brackenbury, the lieutenant of the Tower, while the preparations for the coronation went on. Their mother, filled with unhappy forebodings for them and fearful of her own fate, was in sanctuary at Westminster.

The tale as we have it runs thus: Richard left for the north after sending a plain message to the lieutenant of the Tower. At Warwick, Richard was informed that the worthy knight refused to do his bidding. Nothing daunted, Richard sent orders that for one night only he should give up his command to Sir James Tyrrell. That officer, who lived in mortal fear of Richard, came to the Tower accompanied by two ruffians, secured the keys and the passwords, went down to the Garden tower and sent his ruffians up-stairs. Shortly they called him to see that the work was done. There lay the princes, dead. The oldest account says that one was smothered while the throat of the other was cut. Quickly a priest was called and the bodies consigned to earth. Later this priest moved them secretly, where, no one knew, and shortly after died. As the bodies could not be shown some doubted the death of the little princes, and later we have the claim of Perkin Warbeck that he was one of the princes, escaped from the Tower and marvellously spared. Perhaps he may have been Edward's son, for that king ruined many women beside Jane Shore.

Two hundred years later, while making some changes in the White tower, workmen found underneath the stone staircase near the chapel the bones of two boys, apparently corresponding in age and stature to the princes. Rigid investigation confirmed the guess, and Charles II ordered their removal to Westminster Abbey, where they now lie among their royal kindred in the chapel of Henry VII.

When Henry VIII set to work to get rid of his Spanish queen, and take in her place the pretty maid of honour, Anne Boleyn, he let loose forces which kept the Tower full of distinguished prisoners and gave the axeman much work. The desire for the divorce led him further than he anticipated. When he demanded that he be received as the head of the church, one man, the wisest counsellor of the time, who had held high office and whose talents fitted him to adorn any station, refused to go so far. Sir Thomas More, author of Utopia, statesman and philosopher, after enduring confinement for a few months went to the block and is buried in St. Peter's chapel, though tradition says that his head was secured by his faithful daughter, who preserved it carefully and finally had it buried with her in her tomb.

A mad "maid of Kent" began to prophesy against the divorce. She ordered the king to put Anne Boleyn away and to take Catherine back, and finally began to threaten. When the king acted, he acted vigorously. The maid and her associates went to Tyburn, and Bishop Fisher, just then appointed cardinal, who had listened at least, if he had not encouraged the maid, went to the Tower and soon to the block.

For six years Henry had sought a legal method of freeing himself from his matrimonial chains. Then he took matters into his own hands. On the twenty-fifth of January, 1533, the barge bearing Anne Boleyn, now acknowledged as queen, attended by fifty others reached the Tower, and she climbed the Queen's Stairway, where her impatient husband awaited her. Three years later a barge again bore her along the stream, this time attended by armed men, but now she was landed at the Traitors' Gate, a prisoner charged with adultery, and destined to lose her head upon Tower Green. We know that she bore herself well, protesting her innocence to the last, and winning the pity of all. The story goes that no coffin had been prepared for her and that her body was jammed into an elm chest which happened to be conveniently empty. A few years ago, in restoring St. Peter's chapel, her bones were found jumbled together, apparently confirming the story that she had not been permitted to lie decently buried at full length.

Only a few years later another queen of England came a prisoner to the Tower and a victim of the axeman on the Green. Katherine Howard's hold upon the affections of her fickle lord was no stronger than Anne Boleyn's, and also charged with misconduct she was beheaded Feb. 15, 1542. With her died her companion and alleged accomplice, Jane, Viscountess Rochford.

But the block on Tower Hill outside the walls where the public executions took place was not idle. Wolsey's death of chagrin saved him from the Tower and perhaps from the axe, but Thomas Cromwell, whose devotion to his king had humbled so many, was not so fortunate as Wolsey. Many things combined to lose him the favour of his royal master, but nothing perhaps more than his recommendation of Anne of Cleves as a wife for the fastidious, fickle king. She was so plain and so awkward that the king was disgusted, and in 1540 Cromwell went to the Tower and the block as Edward Stafford, the great Duke of Buckingham, had done twenty years before.

The death of Henry made a delicate boy of nine years king, as Edward VI. If, as seemed probable, he should die without descendants, where would the crown go? Both of his sisters, Mary and Elizabeth, had in turn been declared illegitimate and out of the succession. Mary was Spanish in blood on her mother's side, and entirely so in education and feeling. The young Elizabeth was an unknown quantity.

John Dudley, Duke of Northumberland, who had helped to send the king's uncle, the Duke of Somerset, to the block, again began to plot. Henry VIII's sister Mary, who married Charles Brandon after the death of her first husband, Louis XII of France, had left a daughter Frances, who married Henry Grey, later Duke of Suffolk, and had a daughter whose right to the throne, if Mary and Elizabeth were put away, was at least as good as any. So Dudley arranged a marriage between his fourth son, Guilford, a boy of nineteen, and Lady Jane Grey, a sweet girl of sixteen, whose pitiful history has power to stir a heart of stone.

King Edward died July 6, 1553, and Dudley showed what purported to be his will passing the succession to his cousin, Lady Jane, and next attempted to secure the person of Princess Mary, who had however been warned of his purpose. On Monday, July 10, Lady Jane was proclaimed Queen of England and many great nobles gathered around her. The people showed no enthusiasm. They knew Dudley, and they felt that Mary was the rightful heir. So pronounced was public sentiment that the politic began to gather around Mary, who was proclaimed July 19, and Jane descended from the throne which she had unwillingly accepted, after a reign of only nine days.

Immediately the Tower filled. Lady Jane herself, and her foolish husband, her father, Dudley and his four other sons and dozens of less degree were confined, and the axeman was to reap a bloody harvest. Dudley and his eldest son, the Earl of Warwick, went to the block almost immediately. Robert Dudley, the husband of Amy Robsart, afterward the favourite of Queen Elizabeth, and Guilford Dudley lodged in the Beauchamp tower. Today one sees their names and inscriptions carved in the soft stone and Guilford, perhaps, twice cut the name, JANE.

Mary would have spared her unfortunate cousin if she could have induced her to conform to the old faith, but Jane's Protestantism was too firmly fixed, and she had a will of iron beneath her soft and gentle exterior. Refusing to yield her faith, the Nine Days' Queen went to Tower Green, her husband to

Tower Hill, and shortly afterward her father followed his friends and his children.

The queen under the influence of Renard, the agent of Charles V, began the series of executions for conscience's sake which has given her the awful title of Bloody Mary. Those who disliked either the Spaniard or the old church had good cause to fear. Elizabeth was confined in the Tower for a time, but Mary could not bring herself to order her execution though strongly advised to do so. But Sir Thomas Wyat, Thomas Cobham and then the three bishops, Cranmer, Latimer and Ridley, with hundreds of others crowded the Tower until it overflowed into Newgate and the Fleet.

With the accession of Elizabeth the headsman rested. For a century hardly a year had passed without political executions. During the long reign of Elizabeth they were few, and for twelve years there were none at all. Thomas Howard, Duke of Norfolk, who engaged in the plot to raise Mary Queen of Scots to the throne, was the first; the Earl of Northumberland was mysteriously murdered in the Bloody tower in 1585, and Philip, Earl of Arundel, died on the block in 1595. Nor must we forget Elizabeth's darling, Robert Devereux, Earl of Essex, who died on Tower Green inside the walls in 1601, though the loving but jealous queen was longing to grant his pardon if he would only ask it.

But the grim old walls held many tenants, even if the extreme penalties were not invoked. Margaret, Countess of Lennox, mother of Lord Darnley, and so grandmother of James I, lived in the Belfry until after Darnley's death, when she was released, a broken old woman. Philip Howard, son of Thomas mentioned above, though guilty of high treason in aiding the enemies of his country, finally died in the Beauchamp tower. It was during Elizabeth's reign that Sir Walter Raleigh endured the first of his four imprisonments, this time for the seduction of the queen's maid of honour and his subsequent disobedience.

At the accession of James I Raleigh returned to the Tower, as a concession to Spain, against whose power and influence he had done so much. He was tried, convicted on perjured testimony and sent back to remain fourteen years a prisoner. The cowardly king feared to put the sentence into effect, and so first in the Bloody tower and then in the Garden house he received his friends, studied geography and chemistry, seeking a method to sweeten sea water, distilling his wonderful elixir, and awaiting further evidences of the king's petty nature. The story that in a little dark cell in the White tower his History of the World was written has no foundation. That work was written in the Garden house. On his return from his unsuccessful and unhappy voyage, he lived in the Brick tower for a little while, was then removed to the Wardrobe tower, and then brought back to the Brick tower and tempted to commit suicide. Meanwhile the Spanish court continued to clamour for his blood, and James, crazed by the hope of the Spanish marriage for his son, at length signed the death warrant of, perhaps, the greatest man in England.

The king's cousin, Lady Arabella Stuart, because of her birth spent most of her life as a prisoner of state, though she was not brought to the Tower until after her unsuccessful attempt to escape to France in 1611. From that time until her death in 1615, she was a resident of the old prison.

It is said that James would sometimes come to see prisoners tortured in the gloomy crypt under the White tower, the place where Guy Fawkes suffered after the discovery of the Gunpowder plot in 1606, before his execution.

Executions for treason grow fewer as the years go on. Charles I saw his unpopular minister, Thomas Wentworth, Earl of Strafford, go first to prison and then to Tower Hill in 1641, and the more unpopular Laud, Archbishop of Canterbury, spent many weary months here in 1645, before the procession to the scaffold. Cromwell kept George Monk, afterward Duke of Albemarle, in confinement 1643-46, but during the reign of Charles II there is less of interest, though Algernon Sydney suffered the extreme penalty for alleged complicity in the Rye House Plot in 1683, and George Villiers, Duke of Buckingham, had three separate terms here.

During the short but turbulent reign of James II, the bastard son of Charles II, James, Duke of Monmouth, spent three days in the Tower, begging for mercy, after his disastrous defeat at Sedgmoor. The "Seven Bishops" were confined here awaiting their trial for daring to resist the king's will, and the infamous Chief Justice Jeffreys, captured while attempting to escape, died in April, 1689, while awaiting trial.

After the destruction of Jacobite hopes at Culloden, three Scottish lords, Kilmarnock, Balmerino and Fraser of Lovat awaited trial for their devotion to the old line. The first two were executed in 1746, and the last in 1747, the last man legally beheaded in England.

A few scattered individuals occupy the pile during the next seventy-five years. John Wilkes, the great demagogue, was here in 1763, and Lord George Gordon in 1780. In 1820 seven persons charged with conspiracy were here, but the days of the Tower as a great prison were past.

For many years no persons have been confined within its walls, but every year thousands go to see the Crown Jewels, the arms and armour, the instruments of torture and the relics of the kings. They study the inscriptions upon the walls of the Beauchamp tower, carved by the fingers of men who knew not what the morrow would bring forth, and stand upon the ground where England's worst and England's noblest have stood.